Never forget

Printed and bound in the United States of America.
ISBN: 0-9765658-0-3

Visit **www.nkgproductions.com** for more information.

Designed by NKG Productions
Cover by Neil K. Goodchild
Photo by Casey Conry

ORDER FORM

A DAY IN THE LIFE: SEPTEMBER 11, 2001

Want more copies? It's **easy!** Want to give someone this book as a gift? It's **easy!** Want to sell this book in your store? It's **easy!** Buy in bulk and **save!**

Neil can be reached at nkgproductions@comcast.net

PRICE INFORMATION	**UNIT PRICE**
1 - 19	$8.95
20 - 49	$7.50
50 - 99	$6.25
100 or more	$5.00

ORDER INFORMATION

Total books___X$___(unit price) = total book price .... $_____
Sales Tax (MA. residents only; total book price X .05) .... $_____
Shipping & Handling (total book price X .08) .... $_____
Total amount of order .... $_____

PAYMENT INFORMATION:
Please make checks or money orders payable to Neil K. Goodchild.

SHIPPING INFORMATION:
Name:______________________________________
Company Name:______________________________
Address:____________________________________
City:____________________State:_______Zip Code:__________
Phone Number:_______________________________

Neil K. Goodchild 123 Clifton St. Attleboro, MA 02703

Lynn Catherine Goodchild
May 27, 1976 - September 11, 2001

Shawn Michael Nassaney
July 7, 1976 - September 11, 2001

A DAY IN THE LIFE: SEPTEMBER 11th, 2001

Neil Kenneth Goodchild

FOR LYNN

You are missed every day.

Acknowledgement

Thanks to Mom, Dad, and Melisa for believing I could even when I thought I couldn't.

Thanks to all of my family who have been there for every event, especially Joanne and Carol; Dan and Jo-Ann; Jill, Zack and Nicolette; Janet, Kenny and Brenda; and Eleanor and Connie.

A very special thanks to all my friends who were there from the first minute and have become family. Especially Karen; Sandy; Audrey; Barbara; Katie; Martha; Taylar and Dan (and Lynn and Brady); Meri and Marc (and Corinne and Camille); Christina and Casey (and Molly & Siarse the therapy dogs); The Waterfall Crew - Uncle Chris, Boogsy, Jeffy, and Eric; Auntie Pat and Uncle Dave; Timmy, Chaz and Jake; Stevie D. (my little drummer boy) and the hundreds of others who have spent time, money, blood, sweat and tears to help make a hard time easier.

And another thank you to Audrey Friedman and Carole Simoneau for making sure all the t's were crossed and the i's were dotted.

Contents

A WORD FROM THE AUTHOR

Now that's ironic, isn't it?

You're holding a book written by me and the first thing you see is a section called A Word From The Author. They should be (and are) all my words. However, with that said, I have to get a few things off my literary chest, before I begin my account of September 11th, 2001.

Most of the times referred to at the beginning of each section (or chapter, if you prefer) are generally right. I am not gifted with a photographic memory which, in this case, probably would not be properly regarded as a gift anyway. These events took place three years ago and I have checked with the other people involved whenever I could, but it is highly likely that I am off a bit here and there. For this, I'm sorry. We've all done the best we could, but I'm sure we are wrong by a little. I am of the opinion that I've got it close enough for the purposes of a memoir and I hope you agree. Overall, I have found that when three people see the same thing and wait three years to tell the tale, you get three slightly different accounts of the same event.

For example, my mother and I have disagreed on certain aspects of this account. We both agree on what has happened but, as a specific example, she remembers me talking to her on a friend's cell phone. I remember a friend transferring a call from her office phone to mine.

One of us is wrong, but we both agree on the subject of the conversation, which is the most important part. There are probably a few of these minor discrepancies in this account, I'm sure. However, I would not go so far as to say this book is full of lies. My Mom has checked all of my facts and I don't think there is anyone who knows more about September 11th from our point of view than her. We basically agree on the content of everything in this book and anything we disagreed on was a very small detail. Like I said, whether the phone rang directly to my office or the call was transferred to me is not as important as what we said during our conversation.

I suppose my point is that it's not so much the exact time it happened, but rather what did happen. My family, friends, and I have done what we can to remember everything as accurately as possible and we've had some help from the *9/11 Commission Report* and the internet.

8:30 PM - 9/10/01

Attleboro, MA.

On most Monday evenings my mother and her friend Karen get together for a few cocktails. I don't know when this ritual began but it has continued through the years with rare exceptions. On Monday, September 10, 2001 it changed slightly: they were coming over to the apartment I shared with my sister instead of meeting at my parent's house. On this occasion, not only did I join them but my father and my sister and her boyfriend did as well. This was mostly due to the fact that my sister, Lynn, and her boyfriend, Shawn, were leaving for a week's vacation in Hawaii (Maui to be exact). Karen, my parents and I wanted to see them off.

We ordered Chinese food and toasted their trip. I had some Bud Lights with my father and Shawn. Shawn was excited because his favorite team the New York Giants was playing in a Monday Night Football match against some team I can't remember. It always baffled me how a kid who grew up only a few miles from where I lived could not only be a Giants fan but a New York Yankees fan, too. I suppose it's a Rhode Island thing. Of course, the fact that the New England Patriots hadn't done quite enough to make us all proud for awhile probably didn't make them look any better in Shawn's eyes. At least the Patriots hadn't done anything yet.

But lots of things would surprise me that year.

Shawn, an extremely organized young man, was already packed and ready. The only thing holding him back was the fact that the plane wouldn't leave until the morning. I don't think he minded too much though. His Giants were going to be playing shortly.

Lynn, on the other hand, well... she was a little less organized than Shawn. Actually, a lot less, I think. She was still working on packing. I have a very clear recollection of her standing over the ironing board and getting the wrinkles out of a pair of pants she'd planned on wearing on the trip. I tried to convince her that she should come downstairs and join us but she simply assured me she'd be down soon enough and that she had to take care of these things now because there would be no time in the morning.

There are several things that strike me as unusual about that night. Maybe some little warnings or harbingers, if you prefer. Karen almost didn't come over, but at the last moment decided she would join us. If she hadn't, she would have missed the opportunity to say goodbye. If my parents hadn't come over, I'm sure they'd have wished Lynn and Shawn a wonderful trip over the phone but would have missed the chance to see them one last time. I might not have been there either. At least not for the impromptu party. Although Lynn and I lived together, there were times when we hardly saw each other for days just because of our different schedules. Certainly, it was a little strange that we all gathered for a little "send-off party" if for no other reason than Lynn and Shawn traveled all the time.

It wasn't a big deal that they were flying off somewhere; in fact this was the fourth time that year they'd flown off somewhere together. Lynn and Shawn went to Florida for a college friend's birthday in January. Shawn brought Lynn to London for a few days to celebrate Valentine's Day. They also went to Disney World in Florida during July. Going to Hawaii was really just another trip. For me, someone who was accustomed to living alone, it was another little break where I could have the apartment all to myself.

I still feel guilty about that.

10:30 PM - 9/10/01

Attleboro, MA.

Between ten and ten-thirty my parents and Karen said their goodbyes and wished Lynn and Shawn a great trip. It was the last time my mother and Karen saw them. Shortly after they left, I was ready to say good night and call it a day.

For whatever reason, I can remember watching the special features from *The Family Man* with Nicolas Cage during the half time slot on Monday Night Football. Shawn and my father joined me to watch the trailer and the several deleted scenes. I don't know why I can remember that so clearly when some things are so fuzzy. In particular, we watched a scene where the main character wheels and deals in a tire shop very much like he did in his previous life as a successful business man. When I could bring myself to watch the film again, I was devastated by the scene in which Nicolas Cage begs Tia Leone not to get on the plane. Why we watched scenes from that particular film, I'll never figure out, I guess. It wasn't some act of fate, I'm sure. It was probably just that the film had just recently been released and, subsequently, I bought it. My family and I have tried to find hidden meaning in so many things since Lynn died but we can't always find the connection. I assume some things (if not all) are just coincidences.

Some things are most likely coincidence and some are possibly the harbingers I spoke of earlier. When you look back on things, hindsight is always 20/20. I'll tell you about them and you can decide for yourself.

The strangest thing, in my opinion, is how Lynn and Shawn fought over the plane tickets. They never fought. When they had a disagreement, it was resolved in a quiet, almost business-like way. But they fought over the tickets to Hawaii. Although very little of it happened in front of me, I know the gist of what they argued about was when exactly they were leaving and, more importantly, who would purchase the tickets. When Lynn spotted something she wanted, she'd just buy it and be done with it. Shawn, more thorough, would research what he wanted, consider the options and then buy it based on whether or not it was the best deal and the best product he could get for the money. This is in no way an indication of his being cheap; let me be clear. You only had to spend about five minutes with him to know he wasn't cheap at all. Shawn would break the ice with people he'd just met by buying the first round. He simply didn't believe in throwing money away foolishly just because you didn't feel like putting in a little time, effort and research.

For the life of me, I couldn't remember who won the battle over the tickets but my mother filled me in on the details later. I know

Shawn spent several hours over several weeks researching the tickets. They fought over who would buy them. Shawn argued that Lynn's credit card was high enough as it was without charging a pair of plane tickets on it. Lynn argued that she would and could buy whatever she wanted with her credit card and, furthermore, he paid for too much as it was. Originally, they had decided on August 27th, 2001, but Shawn found a better deal on the internet. They settled on seats aboard United Airlines, Flight Number 175 bound for Los Angeles on the morning of September 11, 2001.

In hindsight, there were several other things that occurred to me after that day that I found to be strange. When we were growing up, some acquaintances from Europe mailed us four mugs as a gift. Each decorative mug had one of our names printed on it. Lynn's broke during shipping. When we were younger, my parents bought us a kid-sized dinner table and two little chairs. When I got older, I inherited the set but I only received one of the chairs because the other had broken. As kids, we had many Christmas ornaments with our names on them, two in particular were hand-made by my mother. Lynn's ornament broke. I'm not an overly superstitious person, but I have come to believe that it was like *someone* or *something* was trying to warn us that Lynn wouldn't need these things. Perhaps the something was trying to get the family accustomed to the idea that the four of us would one day be just the three of us.

Or maybe it was all just a big coincidence.

On the night of September 10th, 2001, after Lynn finished her ironing and packing, she finally got the chance to sit down and relax. By that time, I had relaxed quite enough and was ready for bed. It was eleven o'clock or so when I wished them a good night. Lynn was on the couch and Shawn was resting his feet on the table, sitting in a tan swivel chair that I still have. That was the last time I saw Shawn. "Have a good week," I said to both of them. I added, "I'll see you when I see you."

As I said those words, I was standing under the hall light fixture. The dome had three bulbs in it. When I returned to the apartment to stay by myself for the first time six days later, two of those bulbs had burnt out.

But *that* is probably a coincidence, too.

Right?

4:45 AM - 9/11/01

Attleboro, MA.

I know the exact time they woke up because I checked the alarm clock myself weeks later as I was cleaning out the rest of the things in Lynn's room. It was no easy task to clean the room, but I had help. The first time I went into the room was on September 12, 2001. I had volunteered to see if Shawn's keys were in there and when I found them, I had a terrible little moment sitting on the edge of the bed and crying. Mostly because I knew that this was only the beginning and the room would need a great deal more things cleared out before we were through. Just being in the room left me with a sad feeling because all I could think was that she had only packed for a week but had left the room forever.

Our two-bedroom apartment had a unique set-up. To get to the stairs, you had to walk from Lynn's bedroom through mine. There was no hallway upstairs. Some of my friends marveled at the concept that a brother and sister got along well enough to be able to live like that. We felt it was no big deal. (Although I'm sure walking from her neat and tidy room into the chaos that was my bedroom wasn't easy to take). I am a relatively light sleeper when it comes to certain noises. If it's loud thunder, for whatever reason, I can usually sleep through it. But when it comes to someone tip-toeing through my bedroom, I usually wake up.

Lynn, a martial artist, prided herself on being light on her feet especially when it came to her morning trek through my bedroom. She was frustrated to find she was waking me up when she came through. When we first moved in, I usually said good morning to her as she attempted to sneak through, but when I found out she was so disappointed I was hearing her, I started pretending to be asleep so she could feel better about her sneaking ability.

On the morning of September 11, 2001 I did wake up as she came through. Somehow, Shawn got through silently or maybe he was the one who woke me up but I only saw Lynn as she came through. She was wearing a white shirt and blue workout pants. Her hair was tied back in a ponytail. Basically, she was wearing clothes quite comfortable for flying, since coach seats tend to be geared as little towards comfort as possible.

Downstairs she had her luggage and her "baby-to-go pack." Where she came up with that name, I'll never know, but it was a small bag she'd acquired during a previous trip with my mother specifically designed for flying. It was equipped with the necessities for air travel, she once explained to me. Snacks, gum and aspirin. The snacks were because she felt that airline food lacked the quality she preferred. Gum was essential for when your ears do that popping thing they always do when the plane is reaching cruising altitude. And, aspirin for a headache. Naturally.

She tiptoed through the room with her head down and that was the last time I saw her.

I saw her walk by but pretended to be asleep so she wouldn't think that she woke me up. Sometimes, I wonder why. However, I know that if nothing had happened that day and they'd simply gone on their trip and returned home safely one week later, I'd have gone on pretending to be asleep when she "snuck" through the room. I guess that's how I justify it. It still remains one of those things that keeps me up at night now and then.

My father drove them to Logan Airport that morning. Shawn slept in the back seat the whole way but Lynn chatted a bit. Due to the early morning hour, traffic was light and the trip was quicker than the usual ride from Attleboro to Boston. My father had given Lynn some spending money for the trip and she cheerfully informed him she'd think of him as they bought pina coladas (or some other alcoholic beverages) on the beach in Maui.

That was the last time he saw Lynn and Shawn.

6:00 AM - 9/11/01

Attleboro, MA.

I awoke to the sound of my alarm going off, which was actually just the radio. It was tuned to the Paul and Al show on 94.1 WHJY in Providence. They assured me it was going to be a beautiful day and weather-wise, they were absolutely right. Normally, I'm not what you would call a morning person but it really was a perfect day. Besides, regardless of whether or not I was a morning person, I had to get up early because I wanted to beat the heaviest part of the traffic to Somerville and to get started on work before the office got too busy.

At the time, I worked at M.S. Walker, a wine and liquor distributor in Somerville, MA. I was in the marketing department and was essentially in charge of running a poster printer and creating point of sale material. That particular morning I had a large number of case cards printed (11" X 17" cards that depict the month's featured product and some text that usually describes the quality and/or positive reviews from the wine critics about it) that needed to be glued to cardboard backing.

Unlike my father's trip to Boston, I was nowhere near early enough to beat the traffic, but I could usually get through most of it if I left home before 7:00 AM. The commute wasn't all that bad that morning and I was driving my pride and joy, a 1981 DeLorean that I had bought a few months before and had finally gotten registered after six very long weeks and several frustrating trips to the registry. It took so long to register the vehicle that I promised myself I would drive it for a month straight if I ever got it on the road and that's exactly what I was doing.

Sitting in traffic on Route 93, you have little to do but listen to music and look around. One of the things you see out there besides overwhelming evidence that the Big Dig isn't working, is airplanes taking off from Logan. That was something that sort of faded into the background for me. They were always there, but I paid them about as much attention as I did the clouds.

That all changed after that day. I looked at the planes with increasing sadness and frustration after September 11, 2001. Usually, I try not to look but it doesn't always work that way, does it? The harder you try *not* to look at something, the more you end up *looking* at it. So, for me, as disturbing as the sight of airplanes are and no matter how much I tell myself not to look, I still find myself gawking upward. Sometimes one passed behind the Prudential tower creating the optical illusion that it was flying into the side of the building and I would wait for an explosion. The image of any airplane approaching a building, even one that is safely up in the air, still makes me cringe just a little. Of course, they always pop out safely in the distant sky on the other side of the building and, as a result, I‘m getting over it. Whoever said time heals all wounds was probably right but I am not quite there yet.

In any event, no matter how hard motorists try to make it last, traffic can't last forever. I blame motorists for traffic, specifically the ones who just won't let you in their lane no matter how long you've had your blinker on. In my countless hours spent in traffic, I can see no other cause for the backups. Remember the days and weeks shortly after September 11th? People were much more courteous to each other not only on the road but everywhere. Old ladies were helped across the street. Respect was automatically given not only to current members of our armed forces but veterans as well. People suddenly viewed the police and fire departments with a quiet awe. Everyone hugged their loved ones just a little bit harder. It is a sad shame it didn't stay that way.

I was at work in my office not much later than eight or so as I recall. I was busy gluing the case cards to their backing and listening to the Howard Stern Show. Stern's show, if you happen to be one of the few who isn't familiar with him, is based in New York City.

7:59 AM - 9/11/01

Boston, MA.

American Airlines Flight 11 departs Boston fifteen minutes before Lynn and Shawn's plane. This plane is supposed to go to Los Angeles. In addition to seventy-six passengers there are two pilots and nine flight attendants. Five terrorists are aboard, as well. Apparently, they are more efficient than any of their comrades because they accomplish their mission quickest; forty seven minutes after take-off they crash the plane into the North Tower of the World Trade Center.

Sadly, of the four planes, this one is reported to be the most chaotic. There was a lot of screaming in the background on the recorded calls from Flight 11. As with all the flights, none of us can say for certain what happened aboard these planes. I don't know about you, but my nightmares tend to fill in the details for me.

The alleged leader of the terrorist group was aboard this plane, Muhammed Atta. The fact that the Federal Bureau of Investigation figured out so much about these terrorists so quickly in the days after September 11, 2001 is a testament to their skills. I remember feeling sick to my stomach when I saw the terrorists' pictures in the paper during the days after September 11th. It still angers me that anyone had to look into the eyes of those murderers. There is more hate in their eyes than anyone should ever have. Even with everything that has happened, I doubt I could ever be brought to hate any group of people enough to kill thousands of innocents. The United States comes under a great deal of criticism whenever a rocket misses it's target by just a few feet. It is as if the world has come to believe that, even under the stress of war, mistakes cannot be made. Ever. At least, not by my country. The four planes that were used as missiles on September 11th were not errant bombs, botched intelligence or faulty judgment. Those nineteen men had no intention of hitting military targets. In fact, their mission was to purposely kill as many innocent people as they could.

And they succeeded.

Lately, it seems that all anybody wants to talk about is the failures of our law enforcement, national security and intelligence agencies. Personally, I think they did the best they could. I met an F.B.I agent and a man from the Alcohol, Tobacco and Firearms Agency in the days after September 11th and anyone who says they weren't doing their best must not have met those two guys or others like them. I don't subscribe to the theory that the government ignored warnings That theory implies an awful lot of people dropped the ball all at the same time. All people can screw up some of the time; some people can screw up some of the time, but not everybody screws up all the time. To imply that every governmental agency from the President of the United States down to the airport security people were all looking the other way all at the same time is very unrealistic and quite improbable. Unfortunately, there are many people out there who believe that is exactly what happened. I am not one of them.

8:14 AM - 9/11/01

Boston, MA.

United Airlines Flight 175 leaves Boston with fifty-six passengers, Lynn and Shawn are among them. There are two pilots and seven flight attendants. Unfortunately, there are five terrorists aboard the plane who have no intention of following the scheduled flight path from Logan Airport in Boston to LAX in Los Angeles.

No one can say for certain when things began to go wrong. The current theory is that sometime after the plane reached cruising altitude (or fifteen to twenty minutes into the flight) is when it was hijacked. Again, none of us will ever be sure exactly how things went on board the airplane.

The general consensus is that the terrorists took over the plane and presumably convinced people aboard that they were being kidnapped and held for ransom. I personally find it hard to believe that fifty-six people would just resign themselves to their fate if they were informed that they had less than one hour to live. Cell phone calls made from the plane seem to back up this theory. The people aboard the hijacked airliner most likely would have gone down fighting as was the case with United Airlines Flight 93, if they'd known what was about to happen.

My mother subscribes to a different theory. She believes that most of the noise was made in first class and that most of the people in coach had no idea what was going on. In fact, she hopes that Lynn and Shawn were sleeping at the time of the crash. As much as I wish it happened that way, I believe that it is highly unlikely for several reasons. First, because I have flown before and I know how difficult it is to fall asleep during the first hour of a flight. Second, there is a lot of evidence that suggests the passengers aboard Flight 175 were herded to the back of the plane and I believe it would be difficult if not impossible to sleep through such activity. The third reason I think they were awake was the reported manner in which the plane was flown. In addition to a sudden sharp turn towards New York City, a witness to the crash (a man who was a pilot during the Vietnam War) swears that, from what he could see from the ground, the plane was being piloted so poorly that he doubts it would have stayed in the air for more than a mile or so beyond the World Trade Center if the terrorists had missed their target. In other words, the flight was far from smooth and, therefore, it is hard to believe anyone aboard could have been sleeping.

The terrorists most likely murdered several people and threatened the lives of a select few (most likely holding a box cutter to the throat of a few passengers and/or airline personnel). In other words, I think they were saying something to the effect of "If you try to fight us, we will kill these people. If you leave us alone, they will live." or the terrorist's old favorite "We have a bomb." In my opinion, most people - especially Americans - don't want to make a move that may cause the death of another person, even if it means saving others. I don't know what it is like to be aboard a hijacked airliner and my nightmares are quite enough to fill in the unwanted details but I can imagine what it must have been like. Chaos. Fear. And dread. I think that it is unlikely that people were murdered and that no one attempted to run away from first class and ask for help in coach. I also think that when terrorists altered the flight path of the plane, people in coach would realize that something was wrong and possibly went forward to find out just what the hell was going on.

The F.B.I. was able to provide us with some answers.

Using a compilation of seat assignments and phonecalls (some recorded and some recounted), they were able to fill in some of the holes as to what happened. The terrorists murdered the pilots and at least two flight attendants. A female passenger who was seated in first class was also murdered. The people were herded to the rear of the plane where most of the phone calls were made. One of the mysteries the F.B.I. solved for me was why Lynn or Shawn never tried to call us. The answer is they probably did try. The way the airphones work on United Airlines flights only allow a limited number of outgoing calls at a time. Therefore, it was first come first serve and since probably everyone tried to use the phones at once, not everyone could successfully make an outgoing call.

As far as panic and chaos it seems, based on the background noise recorded during calls from flight 175, that there was limited panic aboard the plane. There were reports of passengers vomiting, but I think that is a normal reaction to witnessing murders like the ones that occurred on those planes. In addition to witnessing grisly murders, the passengers reported that the plane was not flying smoothly. Eyewitnesses on the ground have confirmed this report. So, I think that explains why passengers were getting sick. I feel nauseous just thinking about what it must have been like on the plane.

The terrorists had knives and the passengers had no weapons. There is some evidence that mace or pepper spray were used on some people because of reports of eye irritation. Personally, I'm not convinced there was mace or pepper spray just because I would guess that even in a pre-9/11 world it wouldn't be an easy item to sneak onto a plane. Something like that would have been confiscated by the airport security or would have caused an arrest, therefore a compromise to the terrorists' mission. The nineteen men who carried out the atrocity were nothing if not extremely focused. However, regardless of what I *think* happened, people aboard the planes reported eye irritations and that suggests that mace and/or pepper spray were more than just possibilities. They probably were used. Just because I'm not comfortable with the idea of mace in my sister's eyes doesn't mean the terrorists didn't figure out how to get the chemical aboard the planes. We know they brought knives on board, after all.

While I'm certain that there was an enormous amount of fear, the fact that there was no screaming in the background on the recorded calls comforts me a little. Everyone appeared to be keeping their heads about them. Outgoing calls were made by more or less calm and controlled people. The most surprising fact was that there was a plan being made to take back the plane. Some of the passengers intended to rush the cockpit and take back the plane. Prior to hearing the F.B.I.'s information, I thought only the folks aboard Flight 93 had time to discuss taking the plane back but I was wrong. It is believed that the surviving passengers aboard all four planes were staging a counterattack on the hijackers. Although they weren't armed, they improvised and, of course, they were greater in numbers. Most military analysts would probably tell you that greater numbers is more of an advantage than greater weaponry, although it isn't always the case. Unfortunately, United Flight 175, American Airlines Flight 11 and

American Flight 77 had only a very limited amount of time to fight back. By the time a plan could have been carried out it would have been too late.

In any event, like it or not, none of us will ever know for sure exactly what happened. The plane's black box was never recovered so, in the end, we have very little to go on but some well thought out theories, recordings, and reports from people who received cell phone calls. I met a woman at Ground Zero on September 11, 2002 who told me her husband, a passenger on Flight 175, left her a message on their answering machine shortly before the plane crashed. He told her the plane had been hijacked and things didn't look good. He then told her he loved her very much and not to let this event change the way she lived her life. The message was clear - no matter what happens, don't let these terrorists get the best of us. That was the last she heard from him. I believe that conversation was a representation of the thoughts of everyone aboard the plane, and that we all should listen to that advice. They loved us and please don't let this event ruin us all.

I have also met someone who witnessed the crash from the New Jersey shore. He told me that the plane came in quickly and made a sudden shift towards the building. It was his opinion that the people aboard, even if they saw the smoke rising from the first plane crash at the North Tower, didn't have much time to realize they would be next. In fact, he believes they couldn't have known based on the angle and the timing. Again, we will never know for sure and that might be for the best.

8:20 AM - 9/11/01

Washington, D.C.

American Airlines Flight 77 leaves Washington's Dulles Airport. Fifty-three passengers, two pilots and four flight attendants are aboard. Flight 77 also carries five terrorists who hijack the plane and crash it into the Pentagon in Washington, D.C. The plane is in the air for one hour and seventeen minutes. Like the planes in New York, the black box is never recovered so the information is limited to what we can gather from cell phone calls.

The plane was supposed to go from Washington, D.C. to Los Angeles. The terrorists diverted it back to its city of origin and crashed it into what was arguably the only military target the terrorists attacked. This, of course, doesn't take into account that the Pentagon has many civilians working inside. Basically, if the terrorists wanted to fight their war against the military, they'd have crashed the planes into military bases (there are some in the Washington D.C. area) so I don't subscribe to the idea that any of their targets were military. They had no intention of fighting our armed forces which is why I don't really consider the Pentagon to be a military target. It was just another American symbol that became the target of people so consumed by hate that I simply can't imagine what it is like to be them. Psychologists theorize that these terrorists not only hate us, but also in allowing themselves to be blown apart in such a violent death, they must hate themselves as well.

I won't go so far as to pity the terrorists because they deserve none, but imagine hating yourself that much? That is sad. When they look at their children, do they see potential weapons? Instead of dreaming of a day when junior goes to college, do they look forward to the day junior straps a bomb to himself to kill random people?

8:42 AM - 9/11/01

Newark, NJ.

United Airlines Flight 93 departs from Newark, New Jersey. Thirty-four passengers are aboard, along with two pilots and five flight attendants. This plane also has four terrorists aboard and remains one of the most talked about planes involved in the attacks that day.

Although Flight 93 was not the only plane on which the passengers decided to take back the cockpit, it was the only one where they almost succeeded. No one knows for certain what the intended target was but it was likely to have been the Pentagon or the White House. We know that the terrorists were one man short. We also know the plane was in the air for more time than any of the other planes with one hour and twenty-one minutes of flying time. I think that both of these factors caused them to fail and the actions of the people onboard the plane saved countless lives. Who can say how many more people would have been killed if the plane had crashed into a city instead of a forest?

More information came out of the crash site in Pennsylvania than in any of the other sites. The black box was recovered and more cell phone calls were made. As a result, the authorities were able to put together more definitive information about what happened on Flight 93.

The phrase Todd Beemer used just before he and some other passengers tried to take the plane back became a national slogan - "Let's Roll." Todd was quoted in a speech by the President of the United States and Neil Young wrote a song entitled *Let's Roll* in honor of the heroes of Flight 93. I have little doubt in my mind that we will one day see a huge budget Hollywood movie based on the actions of Todd and his fellow passengers.

9:00 AM - 9/11/01

Somerville, MA.

It was give or take 9:00 AM when Howard Stern received information about a possible plane crash in New York. I listened with minimal concern because his show is plagued with people calling in all kinds of things. He announced it with indifferent disbelief for the simple fact that people make outrageous claims to him very regularly. Stern's show is probably better known for interviewing strippers who have had relations with space aliens more than it is known for broadcasting world news events. He reported that a caller claimed a plane had crashed into one of the World Trade Center Towers. He didn't seem to believe it himself, but did say that if it was a joke it certainly wasn't funny.

At this point, I called my parent's house to ask if there was anything on the news about a plane hitting a building in New York. My father put the TV on and checked a couple stations. None of them had any of the sort of "This just in..." messages scrolling across the bottom of the screen. So, we both decided that it must have been some kind of prank. Stupid, but an unfortunate side effect of the Howard Stern show is stupid people playing stupid pranks in an attempt to get air time. I hung up the phone and the issue was settled in my mind.

Well, it wasn't long before Stern was able to confirm that a plane had hit one of the World Trade Center Towers. Once it was confirmed, I immediately decided that it was no accident. As I recall, Howard Stern felt the same way. How can a plane accidentally hit one of the tallest buildings in New York City on a clear day by mistake? Although it is possible, I had an immediate gut feeling that something terrible had happened and the word *terrorist* immediately came to mind. I don't know why terrorists are so obsessed with planes but, in my mind, the case was settled already.

My father called me back to confirm what I already knew. A plane had hit one of the towers and, furthermore, it was a commercial airliner. Also, reports were coming in that the plane was from Boston. How the hell they knew that so quickly is way beyond my capacity. *Lynn was flying out of Boston today*, I thought. That was when the first wave of adrenaline hit my stomach but I was quickly able to recover. Lynn may have been flying but she left Boston far too early to be involved in this mess. Right?

That was pretty much how simple it was. Denial is such a powerful reaction but curiosity is even stronger. I think everyone's reaction was similar. If you hear about a plane crash, you wonder if the people you knew were flying that day were involved. If the plane has crashed into a building, you'd want to know if anyone you knew was in the building. These simple questions and an overwhelming desire to get them answered are what led to the phone lines being so busy.

Sitting in my office in Somerville, I reasoned that Lynn and Shawn had left Logan at six-thirty or so. If so, she'd be well beyond New York by 9:00. At least, that's what I wanted to believe. I think it's likely that this was just one of the many defense mechanisms that psychologists so often talk about. I figured that anybody who was leaving Attleboro at 5:00 AM would be on a flight around 6:30 or so. And that made me feel better, at least at that time.

But I was way off as it turned out.

And that was when the phone calls really started.

9:03 AM - 9/11/01

New York City, NY.

United Airlines Flight 175 crashes into the South Tower of the World Trade Center. Lynn and Shawn and everyone else aboard are gone in an instant.

A government representative informed my father that the estimated speed was over five hundred miles per hour and that there was no possibility any people could have survived the impact. Presumably, anyone aboard would have been dead before they realized the plane had crashed, assuming, of course, they hadn't already been murdered by the hijackers.

A few months later, my parents received notification that something had been recovered from the vicinity of the World Trade Center. It turned out to be Lynn's credit cards, her membership card to the Y.M.C.A. in Attleboro, and a paper business card she had received from me. The address on the business card was how they found me. Amazingly. although the card had been through a plane crash and the collapse of a building, the paper had only a small crease in it. I have laminated the card to protect it from further wear and tear, but I probably didn't need to since it had survived far worse than I'm ever going to put it through.

How the items survived not only the crash, but also the collapse of the buildings are beyond explanation. The only damage they received from their violent journey was a single crease on the lower left hand side. There was no evidence of melting, no dirt, and no reason I can think of for them to be in as good a shape as they were. We received the cards in an evidence envelope so possibly they were inside a melted wallet that was discarded before we could see it? Your guess is as good as mine. The New York Police were unable to give any answers as to how the cards survived or under what circumstances they found them. They simply said the cards were recovered during the ongoing cleanup process.

The cards would not be the last things we recovered from the World Trade Center site.

9:25 AM - 9/11/01

United States Of America

For the first time since the Wright Brothers invented air travel, all domestic flights are ordered to be grounded.

At the time, I wondered how many lives might have been saved by this, but it seems that the number of terrorists was limited to nineteen men who focused their plans on the Eastern seaboard. By afternoon, I believed that there was a second and third wave of attacks planned which had been thwarted by the grounding of the planes. This appears to have been a completely false assumption, since I have never heard of any other terrorists being arrested that day.

The normally busy skies all over the country become vacant with the only exceptions being military jets and fighter planes. But those were few and far between when you consider that at any given time you can look up and usually see at least one plane in the air.

Shutting down all air travel shows what a large scale effect these attacks had. Unprecedented attacks call for an unprecedented reaction. I think it was one of the smartest moves that could have been made.

Unfortunately, it was the beginning of the end for some airlines. Many of them have suffered financial problems since the attacks. This is one of the victories that Al Quaeda can claim, but a lot of evidence shows that they intended to crush our economy on September 11th. If they intended to crush our entire economy I would say that they failed miserably. Certainly it was a national financial setback, but it came nowhere near destroying our country. It's pretty arrogant of a relatively small group like Al Quaeda to claim they can bring what is arguably the most powerful country in the world to its knees. I guess it takes a bit of boasting like that to get people to pledge allegiance to a group and kill themselves for a cause.

However, they did accomplish several things no terrorist group ever has: They took down buildings, murdered thousands, and they caused all domestic flights to be grounded. If anyone thinks we shouldn't take every threat made against the United States seriously, they need only to look back on September 11th and realize that it took just nineteen men to accomplish a horrifying act of destruction that none of us will ever forget. Nineteen men killed three thousand people in a single day. Never forget that. I have called them a relatively small group and they are when you consider the population of the world they have declared war on. The idea of a relatively small group of terrorists thinking they can take on one of the largest countries in the world is almost laughable, except that the bastards are actually trying to do it. Al Qaeda is very real. They are not a made-up group that doesn't really exist. Some people speculate that they are spread into as many as sixty countries worldwide.

When we react to credible threats by raising the Terror Alert Levels, it is with good reason. It infuriates me that people dare to say these are not really credible threats, but are actually just political games being played. I guess it's easy for some people to say that. If you didn't lose a relative to a terrorist then it's easy not to take the alerts seriously. In my heart, I know that September 11th is not the end of the terrorists' hatred. It is not their last huge domestic attack. I believe they will be back and, if we don't take them seriously, we will have no one to blame but ourselves.

As the President told us, remain vigilant.

Because, like it or not, they are out there.

9:30 AM - 9/11/01

Somerville, MA.

There was a series of phone calls during this time. You can guess what they were about. Once it is determined that a plane hit the World Trade Center and that the plane was from Boston, anybody in my position would want to confirm that it wasn't the plane with the people I knew on board.

One of the phone calls was one of relief. My mother told me the plane that hit was an American Airlines plane and that since Lynn and Shawn were flying on United Airlines, we were OK. "That was really scary," she said with her voice choked with emotion. "We just came that close."

I agreed. I also said that it was shaping up to be a bad day for America. When I hung up, I felt an intense sadness and I am by no means psychic but I swear that at that point I knew something was wrong. Something awful was happening and I knew that it wasn't over yet.

I worked in a fairly large office but that doesn't mean word doesn't travel fast. Moments after I talked to Steve in the office next to mine about what had happened word spread. Soon, word spread that my sister was flying that day. People trickled in to say a few words of support and let me know they were praying that it wasn't her plane.

I'd only worked there for just a few months and some of these people offering support didn't even know me. That was one effect that I imagine Osama Bin Laden never even thought of. Attacking the United States was supposed to bring us to our knees, not make us unite. Never in my life had I seen such overwhelming support come right out of the woodwork. As terrible a day as it was turning out to be, I will never forget the support network that built up immediately, a network that consisted primarily of people who barely knew me.

As I hung up with my mother the profound bad feeling increased. No matter how much I tried to convince myself that Lynn was OK, something inside me was telling me that she was not. There was a lump in my throat that wouldn't quit even after my mother told me that it wasn't Lynn's plane.

Then Stern reported that a second plane had hit the other tower.

My tie suddenly felt really tight. The adrenaline surge reoccured and I remember feeling almost numb as an wave of grief washed over me. *A second plane hit the World Trade Center Towers*. At that point, the little bit of hope that this was just an accident died out. Two planes crashing into the Towers on the same day was just too great a coincidence.

We were under attack.

I went next door to Steve's office again. I told him about the reports of the second plane hitting. I remember saying, “I think we are under attack.”

The concept of the continental United States being attacked in a huge way by determined terrorists from the Middle East was not just a possible future anymore. Pearl Harbor was about to get some competition. Even as it was happening, before I knew how directly my family had been involved, I knew that we were in the middle of a historical event. I already knew that this would be one of those defining moments in life. Where were you when Kennedy was shot? Where were you when the Berlin Wall came down? Where were you when the space shuttle Challenger exploded? Where were you when the planes hit in New York City?

How did I know they were from the Middle East? I didn’t really. I just assumed. When I heard of the bombing of a government building in Oklahoma City, I assumed it was terrorists from the Middle East. You can imagine how surprised I was to find that our own people were plenty capable of terrorism. Blame it on watching too many Chuck Norris films as a child, if you like.

I guess it’s bordering on a racist attitude but in my relatively short life we’ve had far too many events involving terrorists from the Middle East that I can remember. I was a child when the Iran hostage crisis was happening. That was the first time I learned about a place on our planet called the Middle East. There were many attacks over the years, many of them in the Middle East against American interests. Planes had been hijacked by psychos before. In fact, whenever I heard the word "terrorist" I always think of idiots with handkerchiefs on their faces running around planes. There was the bombing of the plane over Lockerbie, Scotland. The World Trade Center had already been attacked by terrorists once. Before September 11th, I'd been enraged most recently by the bombing of the U.S.S. Cole. In fact, I'd argued with a coworker that we ought to go to war. He replied, "With who?" All I had to say was that I wasn't even thirty years old yet, and terrorists had been taking potshots at us for basically my whole life. When the hell were we going to do something about it?

On the radio, Stern was voicing many of the thoughts I had. "I've been saying it for years," he said. Terrorists had been building up to this for quite some time. Now, you probably are going to ask if I think the government could have done something to prevent it? The answer is, not really. Should we have responded more strongly to events in the past? Yes. Definitely yes. Is it possible that they could have been stopped? No way. No chance at all. Even the greatest martial artist in the world can get hit by a suckerpunch. Because it is a suckerpunch. If you ask me, the 9/11 Commission was formed with the best of intentions but eventually turned out to be a group of Monday morning quarterbacks talking about how the game *should* have been played. There are too many people in the world who want to talk about how the game could have been won the day after it's been lost.

There's not enough folks talking about how to win next week's game.

9:37 AM - 9/11/01

Washington D.C.

American Airlines Flight 77 crashes into the Pentagon. An entire fifth of the famous five-sided structure is destroyed. The explosion is heard and felt many blocks away. One of the managers at work has a son who is going to school in the Washington area. Shortly after word gets out that this has happened, he is able to contact his father in Somerville, to say that he is OK.

I believe most people that made those types of calls got good news. Although thousands were murdered that day, countless others were not. Think about how many people live in New York, Washington, or Pennsylvania. Think about how many people were flying that day. I'm certain that there were many calls made that day that resulted in tears of relief. There are a lot of people I know who called each other just to hear the other person's voice. When you see the kind of horror we all saw on September 11th, I think it's only natural to reach out to family and friends.

One positive thing that came out of September 11th is the reminder that we are all in this together. Sadly, we seem to forget that from time to time. Our politicians definitely do. If I could say anything to them, it is that we are Americans first and Democrats, Republicans, and Independent Parties second. Whether for better or for worse, I think most of us would have to agree that there is nothing like a common enemy to bring us all together.

And we certainly do have a common enemy now.

9:59 AM - 9/11/01

New York City, NY.

The South Tower of the World Trade Center collapses.

When I heard about this on the radio, I couldn't believe it. My first thought was that it was impossible, that this couldn't be happening. My next thought was that everyone had to get the hell out of the other tower as fast as they could. Sadly, some of the people had no option of leaving. Those who were caught above the fires could only await their fate and some of them chose to leap out the windows rather than wait.

Terrorists consider a person a hero if they murder people. In America, a hero is the person who runs into a burning building to save just one life. Because America has plenty of heroes, many more people, especially fire, police and rescue workers lost their lives. In the intense sadness that not only I have felt, but also most of the world has felt since the terror attacks of September 11, 2001, I have also felt an enormous sense of pride that I come from a country of true heroes.

Not only did the volunteers and rescue personnel make me proud but also the responses from people after made me proud. We didn't burn the flags of Middle Eastern countries and demand blood; we waved our own flag and cried for peace. In fact, we waved the flag, we attached it to our cars, we saw them on bridges and storefronts and everywhere in the United States. That is the American spirit. Our President did not go into hiding, he went to the rubble in New York City and stood not behind a podium but on top of the remains of a collapsed building with a megaphone in his hand and tears in his eyes. This is something you will never see from Osama Bin Laden. He is always hidden and chooses to release videos of himself with plain backgrounds. George W. Bush didn't hide in a cave with a plain background - he stood side by side with rescue workers and common folks. Bush didn't look at photos and videos of the wreckage - he walked amidst it. The message he sent to Americans and the rest of the world was a simple one. *We are not defeated.* In spite of Bin Laden's best efforts, the United States was not brought to its knees, but rather had its chin lifted, its spirit renewed and its sense of pride revitalized.

10:00 AM - 9/11/01

Somerville, MA.

If I am remembering things right, it was after ten o'clock when the reports were confirmed that we couldn't account for Lynn and Shawn's plane. It seemed that the attack was not over yet. The bad feeling I had in the pit of my stomach returned in full force when something that I had never heard of before happened: the phones weren't working. The phones in the building were fine, the lines were up, but I couldn't get through to my parents' house.

That was discouraging, to say the least. But, like most people, I am able to lie to myself quite well. What I was telling myself was that just because I couldn't get through to the house, that didn't necessarily mean anything was wrong. After all, lots of people knew Lynn was flying that day and, naturally, lots of people would want to check to see if she was all right. I probably made ten phone calls before I gave up. My friend, Martha, came into the office and when I told her what was happening with the phone she offered to start calling, too. I told her not to bother, but she finally got through to my mother after awhile and transferred the call into my office.

This call was a lot more frantic than our last. "There's another plane missing," she said. She checked to make sure she had my work phone number right and we promised to stay in contact until this was all over. That's a funny phrase that we all use from time to time.

When this is all over.

It has never reached the point where it's over. In fact, I'd say it never can. So much has changed in my life and continues to change, that I don't see how this will end. There are too many anniversaries, Lynn's birthday, Shawn's birthday, and, of course, the holidays. Even July 4th has changed from my point of view.

Someone turned on a TV in the meeting room at work. All the channels were covering the attacks by that time. They were no longer rumor, the footage was undeniable. The buildings were aflame and the images of the World Trade Center Towers with black smoke coming out of them is burned into everyone's mind.

Because most cameras were pointed up at the skyline at the time, Lynn and Shawn's plane had a great deal more news coverage. I saw the plane hit and the huge explosion that occurred after the impact for the first time. I'm not much of a praying man but I prayed for the families of everyone involved. The meeting room at work began to fill up as more and more coworkers came in to see what was going on.

I actually didn't spend much time watching. It was easier to concentrate on work than think about what was happening in New York and Washington. Especially since Lynn and Shawn might be involved.

I checked the TV twice in between working on case cards in my office. The first time, I saw footage of what would later turn out to be Lynn's plane. A short time later, I saw footage of the buildings collapsing and heard a news reporter attempt to put a positive spin on, babbling about how at least the Statue Of Liberty was still standing. I remember saying something to the effect of "What a dumbass." I suppose that was the beginning of my being hard on news reporters. Some people were still offering their support because word was continuing to get around that my sister was flying that day and that I might be directly involved in this mess.

I kept telling people that we didn't know anything yet. From what I figured, Lynn and Shawn were two of the many people who were on planes being forced to land at airports around the country. As a matter of fact, my secret fear was not that they were directly involved, but that when their plane was diverted, that possibly any terrorists aboard would flip out and try to create a hostage situation on the tarmac. I theorized that day that perhaps Washington and New York were just wave one of many organized attacks that would work its way through the country. Although I had myself convinced that Lynn and Shawn weren't directly involved, I was worried that they weren't out of the woods yet. I even told some people that Lynn was probably at an airport in Chicago or something and she and Shawn were negotiating a ride back East.

I was wrong.

10:03 AM - 9/11/01

Shanksville, PA.

United Flight 93 crashes in a secluded field. America soon learns that there is a small town called Shanksville in Pennsylvania. What a horrible way to end up on the map.

This particular crash site was the most useful to the F.B.I. and other investigative agencies, not only because the black box was recovered, but because it was what could be called "pristine crime scene." They were able to reconstruct sections of the aircraft and conduct the most thorough re-enactment of what happened that day. As far as I know, all the bodies were recovered for proper burial. In today's world, with advanced recovery methods such as DNA matching, there is still no guarantee that bodies can be retrieved from crash sites like the one in Shanksville.

The wreckage was spread over hundreds of yards of grass instead of spread out over many city blocks. Of the four crashes that day, it was Flight 93 that caused the fewest casualties due to the fact that the passengers aboard fought against the hijackers. There are a lot of things we don't know about what happened on the plane that day but we do know that the terrorists chose to crash the plane when it became apparent that the people fighting back were not going to quit back were not going to quit until they got the plane back. The cowards hiding in the cockpit said something to the effect of, "We must crash it." just before they brought the plane down. No matter what the translation (and it *is* debated) one thing is certain: the hijackers in the cockpit were very scared. And with good reason. The people aboard the plane knew what was going on and, furthermore, they were determined to do something about it. It is believed that the two hijackers guarding the cockpit door were taken down by some of the passengers. When you consider it was two versus thirty or more, the odds were overwhelmingly in favor of the passengers - once they made up their minds, they were going to kick some serious ass. The passengers likely used hot coffee on their attackers and probably came up with some other makeshift weapons. Bravery was their most valuable weapon. The murderers in the cockpit chose to crash the plane instead of face justice when it became apparent that the passengers were not going to let them succeed.

In the months after September 11th I thought about Flight 93 quite a bit. Although for a long time, I intentionally avoided the news, I was drawn to any stories about Flight 93. I still wonder how close the passengers came to succeeding. What if they had had more time? Even a few minutes? People tell me thoughts like that can only lead to a bad place, but I can't help but think them.

Wherever that plane was supposed to go, I am very confident that what the passengers aboard Flight 93 did saved countless lives.

10:05 AM - 9/11/01

Washington, D.C.

The White House is evacuated.

This, as far as I know, is not a common practice. I have seen it acted out before in a popular movie, *Independence Day*, but they only did it that time because the planet was under attack by space aliens. But as far as day to day threats go, the White House is generally considered one of the most secure buildings in the world. This is not so when you are dealing with psychopaths at the controls of a jet airplane.

Sometimes, even now, when I watch the news I get infuriated. The most common question these days appears to be what are we doing to make the country safe against terrorists? Democrats accuse Republicans of not doing enough. Republicans blast back that they've done more than anyone else. Politicians seem to consider the safety of America and its citizens just another card to play when the mudslinging begins. When I watch so-called debates and speeches I am nearly always reminded of school children taunting each other on the playground - a lot of words are said but very little of it really means anything.

The money making film *Fahrenheit 9/11* is just another example of a political game. Politicians (and Michael Moore apparently) like to tell only one side of the story. You can watch *Fahrenheit 9/11* and walk away thinking that America never really wanted to catch Osama Bin Laden just because of the number of troops sent to Afghanistan as opposed to the number of troops sent to Iraq. But that's only one side of the story. The other side is that Afghanistan and its Taliban government had no real organized army to speak of. (At least when you compare it to Saddam Hussein's Republican Guard - they were the fourth largest army on the planet.) If you want detailed versions of what happens when you send large numbers of troops into Afghanistan, you can ask someone from the former Soviet Union who fought there. The War on Terror began in Afghanistan with fewer troops than were sent into Iraq for a simple reason: it was a war primarily fought by Special Forces. Most of our military is not Special Forces. When you hear that side of the story it changes things just a bit, don't you think?

Of course, I'm not an award-winning filmmaker, so what the hell do I know about warping the truth?

10:10 AM - 9/11/01

Washington, D.C.

One of the five sections of the Pentagon collapses.

When people talk about the attacks of 9/11, they usually talk about New York. Flight 93 tends to be mentioned very often, too. But Washington, D.C. was hit hard, as well.

There is no telling where Flight 93 was supposed to be diverted, but it is generally accepted that the target was in Washington, D.C. Our capital city was supposed to be hit twice, just like New York.

10:28 AM - 9/11/01

New York City, NY.

The North Tower of the World Trade Center collapses.

By the time the fires were out, five buildings in all were destroyed. Without question, New York was hit the hardest on September 11th.

Few of us will ever be able to forget the images of Manhattan being almost completely obscured by smoke. Gray ash spread everywhere. Someone told me they'd heard that some of the dust coming down from the World Trade Center site was pink due to the blood of victims mixing with the concrete as the buildings fell. Now *there's* a thought that helps you sleep at night. It was, in every way, a day of horror the likes of which our country has never seen.

Exactly one year later, I walked down a ramp into a gaping hole where two of the world's tallest buildings once stood. The nearby buildings were covered in giant flags and you could see that, even though a great deal of work had been done to repair everything, there was still quite a bit of visible damage.

For nearly a year, crews combed the site for remains and, for my family, it helped lead to some amount of closure. DNA was taken from my parents' saliva and, as a result, the coroner's office in New

York City was able to identify two sets of remains that were recovered from the World Trade Center site. Although we assume that Lynn and Shawn were sitting (or standing) together at the time of their death, Shawn's remains have not yet been recovered. Nobody has any explanation as to why we have two sets of remains that belonged to Lynn and none that belong to Shawn. As time goes on, my hope that anything will be recovered is fading.

Lynn's boyfriend, the kid who used to sit in the tan chair in my living room and talk about the New York Yankees, is gone.

10:30 AM - 9/11/01

Somerville, MA.

By ten-thirty or so, I was in the grip of all-out panic. Eating food had become impossible at that point and I don't think I ate again for at least another day. The word had spread that there were at least four planes involved and nobody knew where my sister's plane was. The theory that she and Shawn had been forced to land in Chicago was unraveling very quickly.

Someone came in and suggested I turn the radio off and I did. I also felt it might be time to loosen my tie and eventually, it came off. My friend Martha was given the unpleasant task of sitting with me until word came in. Although she was accustomed to seeing me smile and joke, she saw something different that day. I cried. I didn't break down and sob, I just sat on the edge of my chair and the tears fell and fell. For a awhile, there was a song on Shawn's website called *I Can't Cry Hard Enough* which is about September 11th. That is exactly how I felt at that moment. There weren't enough tears in the world to relieve me.

Poor Martha had the daunting task of attempting to keep the mood light. She did her best but I was less than cooperative. Any attempts to lighten the mood were falling on deaf ears, I'm afraid. She also tried the "You don't know for sure yet" approach. I can't explain exactly why, but I knew that Lynn and Shawn were gone. I wasn't yet aware that I had actually watched them die on TV (Remember, the news had just started their endless repetition of Lynn and Shawn's plane exploding.) but I just somehow knew they were gone. It was like I could feel them leave me.

So I sat on the edge of my chair and cried until my phone rang. The woman on the other end was Maria, my parent's neighbor across the street. She had just moved into the neighborhood only a couple weeks before. I have to tell you it is not encouraging when you are waiting to hear some good news and someone you've only met once is giving you a call at work.

"Neil?" she asked.

"Yes," I said.

She introduced herself and explained she was trying to get through to me. The phone lines on September 11th were clogged up in a way I had never heard of before. "Hold on just a moment, I'm going to put you on with your mother."

My mother got on the phone. "Hi, honey," she said. She was trying to sound hopeful, almost cheerful. It sounded somewhere between strained and plain old painful. "We need you to come home, but we don't want you to drive."

I asked what happened.

My mother just kept the cheerful/painful voice going. I could *hear* the sadness. "We just need you to come home, that's all. Because we don't know what's happened."

I got angry. I guess that's what happens. You go from sad to angry. I was mad because I could tell she wasn't being honest with me. She didn't answer my question. I was mostly mad because I knew damn well what had happened and I just wanted someone to admit it.

"Nothing's wrong," my mother insisted. "We don't know yet. We just want you home."

I wasn't buying it at all.

"Just tell me what happened," I demanded.

"We don't know, OK? We don't know!"

"You know something!"

My mother broke. "Her plane went down in New Jersey, OK? That's all we know. We don't know if she's alive or dead. We just know the plane is missing and it went down in New Jersey. We're still waiting to hear more."

My guess is my shoulders slumped at that point. I remember wanting to punch a wall or the desk or something but I didn't have it in me to move. I felt numb from the inside out, like someone had jabbed me in the gut with a strong anesthetic that was slowly spreading throughout my body. Whatever control I had left switched over to full auto-pilot. We arranged for a ride. Lynn's godparents lived in Malden and I was in Somerville. They would pick me up on the way to Attleboro.

I can remember holding my green tie in my hands. A tie Lynn had bought me when I got a promotion at my other job. I looked down at it and noticed that my vision had gone quite blurry. It was the tears of course. Martha asked me what happened. I summoned my voice from somewhere inside me.

"Their plane went down in New Jersey," I heard myself say. It seemed impossible. I was saying out loud that Lynn and Shawn were dead.

Even though I heard the words coming out of my mouth, I don't know how they got there. *Lynn and Shawn died in New Jersey. Two kids who, between them, had stepped on almost every continent in the world, from Hawaii to Australia to Germany, England and more. They had been everywhere and they died in New Jersey.* Martha said she was sorry and that she'd stay with me until my ride came. The receptionist was told two people would be by to pick me up.

Later, Martha told me I was pretty calm. I cried but I didn't wail. Although part of me wanted to tear the room to pieces just to vent some of the frustration, I just sat there. If I was quiet before, I was absolutely silent now.

Lynn's godparent's, Connie and Eleanor called to say they were having trouble finding the place. Eleanor was understandably upset. She was asking about where M.S. Walker was located and she was asking if I was sure the flight number was 175 at the same time.

12:30 PM - 9/11/01

Somerville, MA.

Connie and Eleanor called again. There was so much traffic and confusion that they doubted they could find me or get to me anytime soon. In the meantime, Martha offered to bring me home but we had to wait until Connie and Eleanor called again. I later found out that there was a bomb scare on Route 99. Someone told me that, at least. The story was there was a suspicious car and since we had all seen what was happening in New York and Washington, the police were taking no chances. I never did confirm that story, though.

I once had a conversation with Connie about cell phones. Connie, a World War II veteran, believes that they are a waste of money and an annoyance. I think by the second call they had to make to me from a payphone, he was probably figuring that cell phones were neither foolish nor a waste of money. They told me they weren't sure what was going on but that they were stuck in traffic on Route 99 and it basically wasn't moving at all. I assured them that Martha would take me home and that I would see them when they got there.

This sequence of events was very dreamlike. People at work were just finding out that the new guy had lost his sister and her boyfriend aboard one of the planes. I remember people crying, I remember holding my tie in my hands. One man asked me what happened and I had to explain that Lynn's plane went down in New Jersey. I gave the key to my car to one of the higher managers in case for some reason it had to be moved. They assured me the DeLorean would be safe, but it had suddenly lost the high priority status it had been enjoying and I wondered when I would care about the car again. Two friends, Casey and Christina Conry, brought me back to work to pick it up the next day, but it was more so we could have something to do than a desire to protect the car. I had a feeling in the days after September 11th that I would crawl out of my own skin if I sat still for too long. Sometimes I still get that feeling.

I told the receptionist that we were leaving and if Connie and Eleanor did happen to find M.S. Walker, I was sorry but I had to go. One of the managers told me that I could have as much time off as I needed.

The ride home was uneventful. Martha found a station on the radio that played rock and roll and wasn't talking about what happened, which was for the best, I think. I may have said about three words on the ride to my parents' house, but I doubt it. I had been expecting heavy traffic but Route 93 was uncharacteristically clear for the ride back to Attleboro.

Although I didn't notice it at the time, the skies over Logan Airport were eerily free of planes. For the first time ever, all planes in the airspace over American soil were grounded. People all over the country were stranded as I had originally hoped Lynn and Shawn would be.

The ride that had taken me well over an hour to do that morning took far less than that on the way home. In about forty-five minutes we were pulling onto Dewey Avenue and into a blanket of protection that I didn't know was there yet.

1:00 PM - 9/11/01

Attleboro, MA.

It was really a beautiful afternoon. Weather-wise it was a perfect day for a gathering. Maybe a little warm, but not uncomfortably so. My parents have had many parties over the years and as Martha drove me down the street that Lynn and I grew up on, that's exactly what it looked like in front of my parent's house - it looked like they were having a party.

I guess that doesn't sound real good, but that's what it reminded me of as we pulled up to the house. I had two thoughts flash through my head: *How does everybody already know?* and *Oh shit, it's real.* This was no dream. Lynn and Shawn and a lot of other people died. So many in fact that the official estimate wouldn't come out for some time. When it did, it was considerably less than I had feared, but was still a very large number. When you consider how long it takes to read a list of the names, you can get an idea of what three thousand-plus truly is.

I got out of the car and saw my parents coming out of the house. We met about halfway up the front walkway and hugged. I can remember my father's face crumpling and he said, "They got our baby." I knew it was real then. We went inside and that's when I found out the plane didn't go down in New Jersey. My mother told me that

Lynn and Shawn's plane was the second one to hit the World Trade Center. They were sure because it had been confirmed not only by the news but by the airline as well.

No planes went down in New Jersey that day, as everybody knows. As far as where my mother got the information on a crash in New Jersey, she doesn't even remember saying it. My best guess is that the news may have said a plane went off the radar (or something like that) over New Jersey. Over the next couple of weeks, I would learn that the newspapers and television news people would report a surprising amount of inaccurate information. Most disturbing to me was that it seemed that when they didn't know enough about the situation they reported speculation as fact.

The news reported that mace and/or pepper spray was used on the passengers in the plane. This was suggested later by the F.B.I. It is a possibility, but not a highly likely one. Certainly, they didn't use it on all four planes, but the news reporters said so anyway, without even a hint of proof. At the time, I could not get the image of my sister, her eyes swollen from pepper spray, looking frantically for Shawn on a plane that could only be described as a flying nightmare. My friends tried to convince me that we didn't know this for sure. The majority of what I think happened on those planes is just in my imagination, which is unfortunately quite vivid. The most we got out of official reports later was that mace or pepper spray may have been used on some of the people in first class. Since Lynn was not in first class, it is unlikely that she was sprayed with anything, but try telling me that when it's two in the morning and I still can't sleep. It is what I don't know about Flight 175 that disturbs me more than anything else. Thanks to the news reporter's disturbing account of what *may* have happened on the planes, I decided not to watch TV anymore. So, by mid-afternoon, if you were looking for me, you wouldn't find me within hearing distance of a television set.

Shortly after I got home was when I first saw images of Osama Bin Laden. Apparently the Al-Queada leader had issued warnings against the United States. Specifically, he'd said we were "about to learn a lesson." As out of it as I was at the time, I can remember hearing that and thinking what lesson can some guy in who is hiding in the Middle East really teach us? That he can kill innocent people? That he doesn't differentiate between military and civilians? Within a few days, the Middle East released images of people burning American flags and dancing in the streets. My sister was dead and there were people dancing in the streets. I said to people that what terrorists had actually accomplished was to jam a stick in a hornet's nest and if they wanted a fight, I was quite sure they would get one now. I was right, too. Of course, during the war in Afghanistan and later Iraq, we would only hear about innocent people getting killed by the invading Americans. The flag burners and dancers were long gone and it seemed they had been replaced by people who just wanted to live in peace and harmony. Can someone name a single instance in which protestors in America burned the Afghan flag and called for the death of Afghanis? How about burning the flag of Iraq and demanding the heads of Iraqis. When we hear about the atrocities of war, we don't dance in the streets, we hang our heads low and pray that this won't be necessary for much longer. But none of that ends up on the news. None of that will appear in a sequel to *Fahrenheit 9/11*. Instead we will read about committees that spend 20 months to determine nobody saw a suicide attack coming on the morning of September 11th, 2001.

Our tax dollars at work, once again.

So, within an hour of getting home, I saw images of a tall smiling man wearing a turban or headdress of some sort. Other images showed him on one knee firing a machine gun into targets and nodding approval of the weapon. This was the man, the news people said, who was responsible for these attacks. Fool that I am, I actually thought he was aboard one of the planes. Later, I would find out that it was not Bin Laden's style to actually carry out attacks. He convinces people to commit suicide, but runs and hides when the guns are pointed at him. Still, he appears to be considered a hero in his world. These attacks were primarily to teach a lesson, he'd said. I wonder if he still believes that. It seems to me that we didn't have all that many troops in the Middle East before the attacks of 9/11 and now we have a lot of troops there. One of Bin Laden's manifestos (or whatever they are - rantings if you ask me) claims that he wants American troops out of the Holy Land. Ironically, the attacks of 9/11 just about guaranteed an American presence in the Middle East for the foreseeable future. A popular magazine reported that folks in the Middle East considered Bin Laden a hero because he bloodied the nose of a bully. Well, you can't run up and punch someone and expect them to just sit on the ground and whine about their situation. Sometimes, they chase you and want to punch you back. Bullies can be funny that way.

2:30 PM - 9/11/01

Attleboro, MA.

Due to trouble with the phone lines, I was able to attempt communication with another method: email. I had sent several to my parents when I couldn't get through on their phone, partially assuming that maybe they were online and couldn't or wouldn't answer the phone. It wasn't a likely outcome because they had two phone lines, one for talking and one for the computer. However, you would be surprised what you can convince yourself of when you're trying to keep yourself together.

As a result, I sent several emails regarding my situation. My friends, Christina and Casey were on the list. They had just seen Lynn only two days before and knew that she was flying that Tuesday morning. The emails were echoes of the phone conversations, only in writing. They went from cautious optimism, to possible bad news, to possible good news and then the emails differed from the phone calls. From Christina and Casey's point of view they suddenly stopped.

That pretty much meant bad news.

I found out later that they called each other several times, after I stopped emailing them. When they tried to contact me by phone I was unavailable. After some time, they decided to leave their jobs and meet at their house. Call it a bad feeling, if you like. But they both felt that something had gone terribly wrong and that it wasn't like me to say that Lynn and Shawn may be on one of those planes and then simply stop all contact with them, as some kind of sick joke.

So, I wasn't at my parent's house very long when I received a call from Casey. I took it in my father's office.

I'm certain that they must have known something was up when they called me in the middle of a weekday at my parent's house when all of us should have been at work. "Hi," he said. "It's Casey. What's going on?"

"My sister's dead." I then started to cry some fresh tears and it was too hard to say much else.

"Oh, shit buddy." was his response. He and Christina were crying on their end, too. They had just seen her so alive and vibrant less than forty-eight hours earlier. Lynn had picked up one of their kittens and walked around with her. She had pet the dogs, walked down and took a look at the lake, stood by their front door and had a conversation. Lynn's new Volvo was parked in their driveway as she had proudly shown it to them. And, now she had been taken away from us in such a violent shocking way that none of us could really believe it.

We gathered ourselves up enough to agree that they were coming down. Did I need anything? Nope. Just friends. I certainly couldn't eat. Maybe I could drink a beer, who knew?

Speaking of Volvos, my father called to inform the dealership that Lynn had died. She hadn't even made her first payment on the vehicle, not that she hadn't tried. She only owned the car for three weeks and before she left for vacation, she had left the payment in an envelope with a stamp and a note that said, "Please mail this Thursday." I have no idea why my father had to call Volvo himself; we did have a houseful of people. I only heard part of the conversation, but I can tell you that "difficult" would not be a strong enough word for it. I walked away, unable to listen to the rest and frustrated that he had to do it at all. The dealership came and picked up the car, telling us they would take care of all the paperwork and they were sorry for our loss.

3:30 PM - 9/11/01

Attleboro, MA.

As the house filled up with relatives and friends, I attempted to fade into the background. I sat in a chair and breathed. Everything, it seemed, was difficult to do. I had to force myself at times to simply take it one step at a time. For example, walk in the living room... sit in the chair... do not punch the walls.

My stomach was so upset that I could taste it in my mouth. My mother made sure that all three of us had plenty of breath mints, because we all had the same problem. It was an acidic feeling that crept up from my stomach and sat at the back of my throat. I guess maybe it was grief attempting to take an ugly physical form.

While sitting in the chair, I noticed that my Uncle Dan had brought his dog, Donnie. While Dan and Jo-Ann took a ride to Beverly to get my grandmother, they left the dog behind. Donnie was a greyhound, a former racer, who has since passed on. He was a long, thin dog with mostly gray markings in those days. It was the twilight of his life and I think Donnie appreciated that he received a second chance when Dan and Jo-Ann adopted him.

Of course, you couldn't tell that by looking at him. He looked awfully sad and as he was stretched out on the living room floor, hardly noticing the people stepping over him or bumping into him.

off at the wall in a manner very similar to the way I'm sure that I was.

When Casey and Christina arrived, they brought their dog, Molly. In contrast to Donnie, Molly was trained as a therapy dog and visits people in retirement homes and hospitals. I don't think she was trained at the time, but let's just say she had a natural talent for cheering folks up. Molly's instincts appeared to be "How can I make you feel better?" She is a Burmese Mountain Dog and not only does she sit right by your side (and sometimes on your feet), but she looks up at you often to make sure you're OK.

As the house filled up, you can probably guess that the phone rang quite a bit. This was when my mother began her mantra of "It's OK, it's OK." I was sitting in a chair no too far from the phone and it didn't take me long to become annoyed with the mantra.

Every phone call was similar in that the caller asked if it was Lynn. The answer would be yes and then there would be some brief crying and my mother would rally herself with, "But, it's OK. It's OK." It wasn't OK, to me. It was infuriating, saddening, maddening. It was a lot of things, but OK wasn't on the list. I had to leave the room I was so angry.

Later, I found out there was an excellent reason for her mantra. She said she was barely holding it together and when she informed people that Lynn was gone, they'd go hysterical. In turn, she wanted to go hysterical. So, rather than completely lose it and crumple to the floor, she instead told people that it was OK. That was much better than the alternative. And it got us all through the day.

When I left the living room, I found my way to the back room, where many people were watching TV in stunned awe. The news channels had begun their constant showing of what I now knew to be Lynn's plane. You could see it fly in and then explode as it struck the building. It looked like something out of a science fiction film because shit like this didn't happen in real life.

I personally found the image disturbing, but perhaps I was biased. I kept thinking *they were alive up until the point of impact. That is the moment they died. What were they thinking? Were they terrified? Did they see it coming? What did those bastards terrorists do to my sister?* The news channels helped these thoughts along with constant, unending repetition. Over and over and over again, I watched Lynn and Shawn and countless others die. We interrupt this program to show you the death of your sister. In case you missed it the first seven hundred times, here it is again.

Am I bitter about this, you ask?

Yup.

At least, back then. Now, thanks to constant repetition, I have become desensitized to the footage. Sure Lynn and Shawn died at that moment, but since I have seen it no less than a thousand times, I simply can't be emotionally worked up every time I look at a TV. Three years later, it still shows up at least once a week or so. Be it on the TV or on the internet, or some still photos in a newspaper or a magazine. Try to avoid newspapers, magazines, the internet and television all at the same time. Unless I curl up into a ball, pull a blanket over my head and move to the mountains somewhere, it's pretty much impossible.

In the days after September 11th, 2001 I was afforded a small victory when I heard that schools and parents were asking them to ease off that footage just a bit. Seeing as how kindergarteners were taking toy planes and making them smash into walls and desks. It only took the media a couple of days to catch up to my thinking that maybe this was some pretty disturbing shit.

It didn't matter to me anymore because I stopped watching TV in the afternoon and refused to watch it again until October or so. With the exception of Patriot's games, that is. The world may have been falling to pieces around us, but I still had the Pats. Even the Pats had to deal with the tragedy directly because one of their players, Joe Andruzzi, nearly lost his brothers in the World Trade Center disaster. His brothers are New York firefighters and, luckily, survived the collapses.

In addition to not watching the news, I stopped watching all my favorite shows. I used to watch *The Simpsons* re-runs twice a day with Lynn. I stopped after she was killed and didn't watch the show again for almost a year. We also used to watch *That Seventies Show.* I tried to watch it again in October of 2001 but it sent me into such a crying fit that I gave up halfway through. I still don't watch that show anymore, but *The Simpsons* made a comeback in my life when the DVDs were released. By the time the second season was released on DVD (summer of 2002) I started to watch the re-runs again every once in awhile. I'm sure the Fox Network is grateful for my return to regular viewing.

Well, with the living room out of the question and the back room still on endless repetition mode, that left the porch. The back porch gave us the perfect view of the perfect weather on one of America's most violent days in the history of the world. Several people joined me out there and I began getting questioned by some of the people who didn't know me as well as they knew my parents.

"You were Lynn's brother?"

"Were you two close?"

"How are you doing?"

"Isn't this awful?"

You get the picture.

I have only been around for a relatively short period of time. I mentioned that I knew what it was like to live through an event so big that people mark time with it. Like, where were you when Neil Armstrong stepped onto the moon? September 11th was possibly the only time that my whole world seemed to just grind to a halt. The closest thing to it I have ever seen was when the O.J. Simpson verdict was read. I was in college at the time and I can remember that I had to walk around the campus center instead of through it because the crowd was so huge around the TV, There was news footage of people crowded in the streets, quietly watching the television, waiting impatiently for something to happen. That is the closest thing I've seen to the world taking a break to just watch things happen, but it was nothing like September 11th.

More people than I could count took time off from work to be with my family. You couldn't turn around without seeing another sympathetic face or someone wanting to lend a shoulder to cry on or just a person desperate to make some of this pain go away. I think that's how the Red Cross ended up with so much money. So many people across the entire United States just wanted to do *something* to take a step back towards the country becoming normal again.

Remember all the American flags on cars? Remember when we were stopping to let pedestrians cross the street even if we didn't have to? Or let someone with their blinker on into our lane? (Now, there's a royal no-no in the Boston area!) One woman commented that isn't it awful that something like this had to happen to remind us to hug our loved ones every time they leave the house.

4:30 PM - 9/11/01

Attleboro, MA.

Casey and Christina arrived at the house. My mother was asking how many of my other friends knew what had happened. I wasn't sure. She asked me if I wanted to call anyone else, but my answer was no. I did want to call, but I just couldn't. I didn't know what to say. One of the things that people do after an event like this is say, "I don't know what to say." My answer was always, "Neither do I."

By the afternoon, most people either already knew or were about to see the list of names on TV. I really didn't need to call anyone. The three of us had our own way of digesting what had just happened. My mom felt a strong urge to answer every call that came in and assure everyone that it was all going to be OK. My dad and I sort of withdrew and adopted what you might call the thousand yard stare for parts of the day.

As it turned out, there was one person that I was going to call, in spite of how hard it would be. That would be my best friend, Marc. He was going to be given the unpleasant task of spreading the word to my other friends, many of whom were part of his family. However, I didn't have to. By the time I got the courage up, he had already been informed.

Marc was installing the lawn sprinklers at a friend's house. Specifically, Tom and Jane's house. Lynn had babysat Jen, Kristen, Lauren and Emily (Tom and Jane's kids) since they were very little. So, when Tom found out he went home and found Marc and his crew working in the yard. He called Marc over and told him the news. Not an easy task, I can assure you. In doing so, he saved me from one of the more difficult parts of the day.

So, shortly after Casey and Christina arrived, there was Marc. Soon, there was Meridith (Marc's wife who also left work to come see us). The porch filled with more people who knew me and I know now that more than one of them was hoping their normally goofy friend Neil wasn't about to change permanently.

It was around this time in the afternoon that we all started on the beers. Like the food and drinks that were already there, the coolers full of beer also appeared like magic. When I say we had a houseful of support, I really mean it. They thought of everything.

Now, some psychologists would probably balk at the concept of drinking during a time of sorrow. Actually, most of them would, I'm pretty sure. My mother flatly refused to drink saying, "I only drink in times of happiness." Well, as for me and some of my friends, we all had a few beers. Maybe more than a few. You can call it an improper coping mechanism, if you'd like (It's a free country). But one thing even a psychologist will admit - it's better than not coping at all.

Everybody has different ways of dealing with tragedy. Sadly, some people brought shame to our country by committing acts of violence against Arab-Americans and, in some cases, people who simply looked like Arab-Americans. On Howard Stern's show he asked people not to do this when he first heard of the reports that cab drivers were being pulled from their cars on the streets of New York. Of course, I don't condone it (Random violence was never my thing) but I guess I can understand the anger. I had to go out and buy a punching bag during the first year, so I'd be lying if I said the whole thing didn't piss me off to the point of wanting to pound on something.

There were no punching bags on my parents' back deck, though. We made do with beers and some idle talk. I know we talked about how the whole world was about to change. At the time, it was reported that as many as ten thousand people might be dead. The only certain casualties being reported were from the airplanes. News reporters like to throw around the word "alleged" a lot, but there was no alleged about the well-documented plane crashes. They were quite definite.

So the conversation on the porch varied from the questions I told you about and some theories on how the country would react to this.

The general consensus was that if a man like Osama Bin Laden wanted a fight, he was about to get one that he would never forget. Overhead, there was the chillingly empty blue sky. Try looking up sometime if you are ever between Boston and Providence (as Attleboro is). Between Boston's Logan International and Providence's T.F. Green Airport there is never a shortage of planes in the air over Attleboro, but that day, there were no planes at all. Anytime you looked up at the sky that day, you'd see a confirmation that all was not quite right with the world.

6:00 PM - 9/11/01

Attleboro, MA.

With a full house and a beer or so in me, I was probably feeling as comfortable as a person can when your world is picked up by the heels, turned upside down and given a good, hard shake. It was late afternoon when the press first began to arrive. I can't remember if we had a discussion about it or if it just worked out that way, but we agreed not to speak to the press.

But they did not agree to stop trying to speak to us.

During the day, we frequently received calls from various news organizations anywhere from national to local. They all got the same answer, "The family is not granting interviews." One of the more disturbing things that happened is my mother actually received a call from a reporter before the airline had even confirmed Lynn's plane had crashed. I don't know who it was or how they did it, but that is the last way you want to get confirmation that the plane your daughter was on has crashed. Apparently, whoever it was wanted the exclusive interview. Imagine the caller's disappointment when they were informed that we hadn't heard from the airline yet. It's hard to comment on the death of someone that you aren't really sure is dead yet.

But when phone calls fail, what better way to get at the grieving family than to jam a microphone in their face on the doorstep?

You have seen it many times on the news. People sobbing and talking about why me and how can this happen to my family and why do bad things happen to good people and etc. It always sounds the same because what you are hearing is raw emotion. Everyone feels that way when they first hear about their loved one getting murdered, trust me. Check around if you don't believe me.

I knew I didn't want people to see film of myself blubbering all over the TV. So, we turned the reporters' ground troops away the same as we did the audio assault over the phone. However, we had help with the ground troops. Our friends formed a tight protective blanket that allowed no microphones or cameras through.

To their credit, only one reporter gave anybody any lip, so to speak. When this particular reporter was turned away by a family friend he whined, "Aw come on, lady, I'm just trying to make a living." You know who you are. To the rest, I thank you for your understanding.

Now, at this point, I'd like to clear up my feelings on reporters. I don't hate them. I agree that even though he could have dealt with the rejection better, the Whiner was right. They do have a job to do in what is arguably one of the most competitive fields in this country. Furthermore, I have spoken to a couple of reporters since that day and I have to say that ninety-nine out of one hundred times, they are simply given the order to go in and do a story. Whether they want it or not is not a choice if they want to keep their jobs. One reporter, speaking off the record, informed me that most of the times you get an assignment like sticking a microphone in a grieving person's face, you don't want it but you still have to do it. Even I have to admit, it's like a car accident on the side of the road: you don't want to look but you have to. That stuff does get people to watch the news. It does get people to buy magazines and newspapers.

Hell, I'm writing this book because people keep asking these questions, I may as well provide some answers.

So anyway, I don't hate reporters. But I do wish I could have been spared some of the footage of the crash. It would have been nice to sit outside my parent's house in relative peace and quiet. It would have been nice to answer the phone and not have someone on the other end starting with, "I'm from the such and such paper, and I was wondering if you could answer some questions."

Something I found to be almost comical was the desperation of the reporters. One went so far as to quote my father in the paper as saying "We have no comment at this time." Even when you give them nothing, they will find something to print. I suppose when you are paid by the word, you have to fill in the white spaces with something.

In spite of my frustration with the reporters I have to admit they are clever. They got pictures, addresses and put together stories that were on the front page of most of the local papers without speaking to us. Shawn's family talked a bit, so I guess that helped. I went from a person who was completely unknown to a guy who appeared on the front page of three newspapers (that I know of). Lynn and Shawn's picture was in *Newsweek*. Their names are on lots of internet sites. If you do a Google search on Lynn's name you'll get about two thousand hits, even now. Shortly after 9/11, my parents eventually ended up on every network in our area because they started talking to the press.

Personally, I kept waiting for the attention to die down. However, I ended up granting an interview to not only the local paper but also a local news station about two years later. If you had told me I would still be getting asked about my story three years after Lynn's death, I wouldn't have believed you. The attention has never really died down.

Because I am on the inside looking out, I don't see the interest others have in the families of the 9/11 victims. I wonder what the difference is between Lynn's death and, say, a person who is killed in a car crash. The obvious answer is there is a difference between accidental death and murder, as far as media attention. That much I am positive about.

From my point of view, when someone dies, that empty chair at the table is just as empty if they've been murdered, killed in an accident or died quietly in their sleep at a ripe old age. Death is death. You will never see that person again no matter how she died. I have gone to wakes and funerals and when I express my sympathy to people, I have been told several times, "Oh, but it's nothing like what happened to you." Maybe someday I will understand what they mean but I don't think that day is coming anytime soon. In my heart I know that losing someone - no matter how - will always hurt the ones who are left behind.

7:30 PM - 9/11/01

Attleboro, MA.

As sunset neared and the temperature began to cool down, the flurry of activity started to slow. Of course, more phone calls came in, more folks showed up. More family members were notified and, as a result, they called us.

At the time, I was too numb to know what was really going on outside of my parents' raised ranch. Somewhere in the back of my mind, I'm sure I was wondering how all these people were finding out what had happened. They found out because names of the victims were being run on the news.

I mean, talk about "we interrupt this program."

I doubt many soap operas showed on the major networks that day. The names of the victims were scrolled across the news shows pretty regularly. Even as I tried to avoid the news, I found myself drawn in to watch as the list of names which included Lynn Goodchild and Shawn Nassaney rolled slowly from the top of the television screen to the bottom. It was all very surreal and it didn't matter if I was ready to accept it or not, because there were the names, like it or not. I suppose it's part of the reason why I resented the press so much. They made it all so damned real and undeniable. I think some late edition newspapers were carrying the names of victims and I'm sure the internet had some lists as well.

As awful as it was for me, I felt almost relieved that at least I knew it was over. When buildings collapse and there is nothing less than complete and total chaos, many people are lost in the shuffle. I remember the Oklahoma bombing well enough to recall that there was some hope that people may have survived the collapse. In the days after the Oklahoma bombing dogs were used to search for people. The dogs became depressed as the days went on and few survivors were found. I can't imagine what it was like in the days after September 11th when the list of the missing was narrowed and the list of the dead lengthened. We at least knew that Lynn and Shawn were gone right away. A plane that crashes into a solid object at five hundred miles per hour leaves little doubt in one's mind. Some of the people inside the buildings had a chance to get out. Many families had to wait for days, with hope becoming more and more distant, before they got their answers. Some had to wait much longer than that.

As things slowed down at the house, some people started to return to their homes to see their own families. Not all, of course. In fact, some of them stayed at our house for days, even if it meant sleeping on the couch just to be there for us.

Many of our friends and family members stayed with us or near us within the first few weeks. That "protective blanket" went up around us and protected us from more than just the occasional pushy member of the press. There was always someone there whenever I needed somebody.

People often ask, how did you do it during those first couple of days?

I think it was easier during the first few days. I was kind of numb. There were people everywhere. In a weird way, seeing that everyone was hurting made it easier for me to deal. It's hard to feel alone when you're surrounded by people. I was hurting and everyone around me was hurting.

It was also quite busy. We had two wakes and two memorial services to attend to. The lines at the wakes were unbelievably long. After Shawn's wake I returned home and there were two rainbows in the sky over my parents neighborhood. One seemed to start at the window to Lynn's former bedroom and end somewhere in Pawtucket (where the wake was being held). That may seem a little dramatic but allow me the liberty because I wasn't the only one who saw it that way. We have several pictures of those rainbows, but none captured the exact angle I saw it from.

I don't need a picture to remember it.

9:30 PM - 9/11/01

Attleboro, MA.

Time has a way of slowing down and then speeding up. The sun went down as it always does, but I didn't notice. It seems that suddenly we were all sitting on the back deck in the dark. Although the day was what you might categorize as emotionally exhausting, the concept of sleep was impossible.

I took a walk around the house a couple times. I would move from the deck to the front stairs. On the front stairs I could see people as they came into the house. I sat with people I hadn't seen in years and drank beers that I couldn't feel the effects of. Someone tried to make me eat, but I doubted I could keep it down.

"I'll eat when I'm hungry."

"Well, you have to eat something. Please try."

"I will," I said. "When I can."

In addition to not feeling the effects of the beers I drank, I couldn't feel any of the hunger that I should have had. I didn't eat breakfast that morning, so the last meal I'd eaten was the Chinese food twenty-four hours earlier. Physically speaking, I should have been hungry. It defied most of what we know about the human body that I wasn't even feeling small pangs of hunger.

Truth be told, I don't remember when I started eating again. I don't think I ate anything that night. I may have had some bread or something, I can't remember.

It was hard to believe that only twenty-four hours earlier, we had all been sitting together. Was it that long? I remember looking up at the clear sky filled with bright stars and wondering how so much could change in such a small amount of time. From a normal Monday to a Tuesday we would never forget.

The sky remained eerily free of planes. When you look at the sky over Attleboro at night, it's usually just as busy as it is during the day. You can't see the vapor trails behind the tiny planes, but you can see the blue and red flashers on the bottoms of the wings.

Either way, I have never looked at a plane the same again and never will. Airplanes are no longer just a means of travel. They have become weapons - missiles with innocent people aboard. My parents flew several times before Christmas, but it took me almost two years before I got on a plane.

I never liked flying much even when planes weren't potential weapons.

11:00 PM - 9/11/01

Attleboro, MA.

I wasn't tired, but the time when people normally go to bed made me wonder when I would be able to sleep normally again. Starting that night, dreams made sleeping difficult. At first, they were just dreams that tried to convince me that none of this ever happened. Lynn was still alive in my subconscious. When I would wake up, I'd realize that real life was the nightmare.

There were nightmares in the months after. There are still nightmares, even now. I no longer fear monsters in the night. I dream of terrorists on planes. I sometimes dream of terrorists in the woods around my house, closing in on me. The worst nightmares I have are when I catch them and I realize that I am the monster. I have done some terrible things to the terrorists in my dreams.

12:00 AM - 9/12/01

Attleboro, MA.

My father and I were in the kitchen. It was starting to get really quiet around the house. When it gets quiet like that, the only thing you can hear are your thoughts. After a day like September 11th, you don't want to listen to your thoughts for too long. Raw emotions are arely good for the psyche.

It was dark outside. The house looked similar to any house that as just had a party. My father was crying and wondered aloud if here was something he could have done to prevent this. He had ropped them off. Was it his fault that this had happened?

I assured him that it wasn't.

My father told me he gave Lynn and Shawn some money before ey got out of the car. A little spending money for the luau they were upposed to be attending after they got to Hawaii. Lynn had smiled nd performed a quick hula dance as she thanked him. "We'll think of ou tonight," she'd told him. My father shuddered with a quiet sob as e both realized they were supposed to be doing that right now.

"It's not your fault," I repeated. "You can't even talk like that." ynn and Shawn were murdered. My father didn't bring them to the rport to have them killed. They didn't buy the plane tickets and ook the hotel to get themselves killed. This whole thing was the fault of people who spent most of their lives in a country I never thought about, training to kill people they would never know.

Do you ever stop and think about how strange the concept of terrorism is? There are so many contradictions in a terrorist's behavior They think they are patriots avenging the lives of innocents but the people they strike at are innocents themselves. How can you purposely target people you can't possibly know? How can anyone do that? It's incredibly disturbing to me that anyone could be capable o such hatred. I don't even like to kill the spiders I find in my showe sometimes and these people cheerfully blow themselves to smithereen just for the chance to kill an American.

Show me what an American is. Tell me what color an American' skin is. Tell me what religion an American is. Are all Americans rich Are our streets paved in gold and lined with diamonds? The answe is not so simple. Americans come in all shapes and sizes, all religions from every country in the world, from every background you ca think of. It's not a simple definition.

We wouldn't have it any other way.

The only people in the world who can categorize us as an inherently evil bunch of people are terrorists. The rest of the planet smart enough to know that, like snowflakes, no two Americans ar alike. This country is the melting pot and I am proud of that. The is no amount of planes that can be crashed or buildings that can be destroyed that will ever change that.

We have always been and always will be proud to be Americans.

Can a terrorist say that?

Take your average terrorist. He believes he's doing what's right for his religion. But nine times out of ten, they kill some people with the same religious beliefs as they just for a chance at killing one American. And many Americans have the same religion as these terrorists. Terrorists hate everyone with extreme prejudice. If you so much as stand next to an American, you'll be targeted, too. Look at the statistics. The hijackers (nineteen Muslim extremists) killed over three hundred Muslims on September 11th. How can they justify that? It's one thing to claim you must kill infidels, but it's another thing altogether to start killing the faithful just for being near the infidels. How the hell do the Al Quaeda recruiters explain this to potential operatives?

I hope I never understand how these people think.

12:30 AM - 9/12/01

Attleboro, MA.

My mother, Eleanor and Connie couldn't sleep any more than I or my father could, so they sat down and made a list of how many people came by the house that day. It totaled eighty-six people - our family, friends and neighbors.

They are all family now.

1:45 AM - 9/12/01

Attleboro, MA.

On an air mattress placed on the floor in Lynn's old bedroom, I attempted to try to get some rest. It didn't work very well. I tried to read a book, but I couldn't concentrate. At some point, I gave up on the book and simply turned the lights off. I stared at the ceiling and cried occasionally. The next few days would be tough ones, I already knew that.

I have no idea what time it was when I finally got to sleep, if you could even call it sleep. I think my body just shut itself down in the interest of self-preservation.

6:30 PM - 9/14/01

Pawtucket, RI.

Shawn's wake.

How do you go to the wake of someone so full of life? He always had a bright smile. He was energetic. An over-achiever, really. Someone I just don't have the energy to even compete with.

I have been to many wakes. I have never cried so uncontrollably just at the sight of the family as I did that day. *They* were asking *me* if I would be all right. I guess that says it all.

The line was around the corner. The streets were wet with rain, but I didn't get rained on. There were so many people there that four hours was not enough to see them all. The funeral home had to extend the time.

Drained, I returned to my parent's house and witnessed the giant rainbows I told you about earlier.

Saturday - 9/15/01

Pawtucket, RI.

Shawn's memorial service.

Part of the reason Shawn's service was so hard was because it was like a practice run for Lynn's memorial service. It's selfish, I think, but in the back of my mind all I could think was *as bad as this is, it will be even worse for me at Lynn's wake and memorial service.*

Shawn's brothers, Pat and Ryan, spoke. They both did an awesome job. Shawn's coach spoke. He had three co-workers talk about him.

Ryan began with a joke, saying that part of the reason Shawn was such a fast runner was really due to the fact that he had two older brothers who would pummel him if they caught him.

Shawn's coach talked about how Shawn could rally the team. Once, in a meet they had won, he convinced the team to throw away the trophy, because although they had beaten the other team, they all could have done better. That was just the way he was.

Shawn's coworkers from APC, a competitive bunch, all had a bet that each of them wouldn't cry during their talk. None of them won the bet.

Lynn's best friend, Taylar, had to leave early because she was eight months pregnant and had what she thought was the beginning of labor. The baby wouldn't come along for about another month.

When it was over and we were all walking out, the song "Forever Young" was played. I never realized how sad a song that could be.

4:00 PM - 8:00 PM - 9/16/01

Attleboro Falls, MA.

Lynn's wake.

We were at Dyer-Lake Funeral home, a place my mother had told me she wanted her own wake to be someday. It's a place I drove by countless times in my life and never gave it a second thought. Now, when I pass it I can only think of one wake in particular.

The hot weather returned in full force. Many of the people coming in were covered in sweat from the intense heat outside. The line was so long, it ended up on the news. Before anyone could get in, they had to pass by an honor guard of two United States Marines.

We stood near a table that had been set up with pictures and mementos. You see, at this point, we had no remains and actually I never expected there to be any remains, but I was wrong.

In some ways, it was a long four hours. In other ways, it flew by. I had no concept of time, but my lower back became sore after a while. We never sat down during the wake. There was no break in between groups of people - there was a line four the entire four hours. My shoulders were moistened by tears and spattered with makeup by the end. Mascara mostly. Eye makeup wears off easily with tears. I started off wearing a white shirt and went home with several colors added to my shoulders. I remember that my hair was too long and I should have gotten it cut, but I just didn't. In the days after September 11th, I didn't stray far from my parents' house for two reasons: I didn't need to and I didn't want to. The hair dresser was way too far from my their house.

My mother had a picture of Lynn in a goofy pose. She would show it to people who were really sobbing. There were many instances in which I lost it myself. You see people crying who are normally happy and that just tends to be the reaction. When the little girls that Lynn used to babysit for arrived, I had a hard time looking at them. I hugged each one and assured them that they still had a babysitter but they would not be able to see her anymore. My friend's father, a gentle giant, was shaking with tears when he came through. He told me later that he and his wife were crying over September 11th even before they knew Lynn had been killed. Many people from work, folks I had only known for a short time, came to see me and my family. As the people walked through I had so many thoughts I can't begin to remember all of the them. The worst of it for me was when kids came through the line. How do we explain a day like September 11th to kids? I guess I will find out someday but I haven't had to do it yet.

At the end, I stood with Taylar. Lynn and I grew up with her. There was a bond between the three of us that words can't express, so I won't try. Taylar and I stood next to each other and stared at what was on the table. Tears fell and we shook our heads. Who would ever have guessed that something like this would happen? Who would ever have guessed that we would be standing here at the end of a long, long day and we would be looking at a table covered in framed pictures, stuffed animals, poems and notes because there was no body? The baby Taylar was carrying would never meet Lynn but she would be named after her. Lynn Taylar McDonald was born one month and one day after Lynn's death. It was fitting because my sister and Taylar were born one month and one day apart.

Monday - 9/17/01

North Attleborough, MA.

Lynn's memorial service.

One week earlier we were toasting Lynn and Shawn's trip, now we were having a memorial service instead of a funeral because Lynn's remains were not yet recovered.

This one I have a hard time remembering. I was in kind of a daze for it. It was very well-documented, I can assure you. I can watch a tape of it if I want to.

So far, I haven't watched the tape.

The house filled up with people again. My relatives came in from all over the country. My uncles, Bruce and Bob, flew in from California on the same plane as my cousin Lorraine and her fiance Tom. They didn't know it until they got to T.F. Green Airport. Their plane was supposed to go to Washington, D.C. but was diverted to Providence just for them, so they could be with their families. Another uncle, Jeff, and my cousin Jameson came up from Florida. My Uncle Kenny, my mother's brother, and my Aunt Janet came up from North Carolina. He drove the whole way because he couldn't wait for the planes to be allowed to fly again.

In the church Lynn and I went to as children, I found myself sitting in the front row trying to figure out how we could say goodbye. The service was nice, at least the parts of it I can recall. "God is crying," Father Graziano said. I think we all can agree on that. None of us can make sense of the tragedy, but I think religious beliefs help. On the flip side, I have heard many people ask what God could allow something like this to happen?

You gotta have faith, man.

Sometimes, that's all we have to go on.

Family and friends did the readings. They did remarkably well. That's not an easy thing to do and there was no way I could do it, that was for certain.

Another family friend, Audrey read the eulogy. I remember most of it but I should because I helped write it. How do you sum up a life in a couple of pages? We touched on everything we could think of.

Lynn was management material from a young age. You could tell that when she was a little girl. She gave orders to people twice her size and somehow got those people to follow the orders. Even as an adult, most people were still twice Lynn's size. At 5'5" and a little over a hundred pounds, she wasn't going to force many people to do her bidding with physical strength.

She didn't need the muscle.

Lynn had attitude.

She also had a wonderful sense of humor. She loved the comedy of

Mike Myers. Her favorite films were the *Wayne's World* movies and the *Austin Powers* series. Unfortunately, she only saw the first two of Austin's adventures. I was probably the only person in the theatre who was sad at *Austin Powers in Goldmember.*

Lynn was a huge *Simpsons* fan. Particularly, she was a big fan of Homer Simpson. She knew most of his more famous lines by heart and we used to repeat them back and forth all the time. When we were at work, we'd email them to each other. Lynn got such a kick out of Homer singing "We Built This City" to a group of college kids at Spring Break that I have adopted the song as a sort of theme for any party I go to. This bugs the crap out of people, but Lynn would have laughed at that, too.

Of course, I can't talk about her favorite cartoons without bringing up another favorite. She loved *Spongebob Squarepants*. It took me quite awhile to get used to Spongebob and his starfish friend Patrick's antics, but once you get accustomed to him, he's not so bad. Every weekend, she watched him whenever she could. Spongebob's view on life and trusting nature is something we should all pay attention to.

She was an understanding person. Always someone you could go to. No matter what was going on in her life, she found time to listen to my problems. Even when she was a world apart staying in Sydney, Australia during the 2000 Olympic Games she coached me through frustrating days at work. Those were weird conversations because there was a fifteen hour difference in the time. So, she'd call and it would be early evening here and mid-morning (the next day) there. We joked that she had traveled into the future to go to Australia.

She was an attractive girl. I don't think she ever had the sort of problems most of us have, trying to get to know people. People had a way of getting to know her. Many of my friends describe her as the kind of person who had an effortless grace. Lynn was the type who had the movie-star looks that went along with being a model, but never had the desire to bother becoming a model. "They can't eat Taco Bell whenever they want," she once said.

So was she a junk food junkie? Well, maybe not a junkie but she liked the kind of food that most people would say is bad. Lynn and Shawn would sit and eat nachos before they went to the gym. She surprised coworkers by eating a lot of pizza and putting down a lot of beers one night. "Where the hell is all that stuff going?" one of them mused while they sat at the bar after work. She was a small girl but, like most small people, a force to be reckoned with. Especially if it was celebration time and beer was involved. Her drink of choice was Bud Light on draught because she had stomach problems and she didn't care for "all the bubbles."

We definitely had different choices in music. She liked rap and kept up with the new stuff. But the show she listened to more often than not was Storm and Burnsie's program on FM 104.1. While it was a different station than my favorite, both stations were not opposed to a crude sense of humor and neither of our preferred radio stations did the sugary sweet crap you hear on some popular stations.

Shawn was a huge U2 fan. As a result, he ended up with tickets for U2's visit to Boston's Fleet Center. They both went to the show in June of 2001. Lynn returned home a born again U2 fan. She was really impressed with "Where The Streets Have No Name" and some other songs that we'd all been hearing for years on the radio, but sound so different when you see it live.

"Where The Streets Have No Name" made an emotional re-appearance in my life when, during an incredible half-time performance at Super Bowl XXXVI, U2 played the song and lead singer Bono shocked us all by revealing an American flag sewn into his jacket at the end of the show. As the song was performed, the names of every victim of September 11th were raised up on a banner behind the stage as well as being flashed all around the stadium. "Lynn Goodchild" appeared large as life during the nationally televised show. I was fortunate enough to see it live, but I also have the show on DVD. Most of the time, I'm not interested in the halftime show of the Super Bowl, but the rumor was that U2 would do something really spectacular and they delivered. I look forward to more half-time shows like that one so we can all forget the infamous "garment malfunction" that made a mockery of one of the biggest events in the world.

As if U2's unprecedented half-time performance wasn't enough, our favorite home team (and major underdogs) shocked America when a twenty-four year old untested quarterback led the New England Patriots to victory over the number one offense in the NFL in an incredible, heart-stopping game. The red, white and blue won in the end, in spite of impossible odds against them.

Was Lynn a Pat's fan?

Yeah, of course.

We grew up watching the Patriots do... not so well. So, it was with great pride that we all shared in the victory of the New England Patriots. It seemed only fitting that at a time when America was feeling low, a team that proudly called themselves the Patriots and wore the colors of our national flag took the trophy home.

Shawn was a Giants fan, so in the interest of keeping him on his toes, Lynn stayed informed of the Patriots sometimes unimpressive win/loss stats. I'm absolutely certain she would have enjoyed the Super Bowl that year. But, as it turned out, she was a part of it, instead.

Getting back to who she was, I would say that Lynn wasn't much of a morning person. She sometimes overslept. Typically, she slept as long as she could provided it was still mathematically possible to get to work on time. Usually, she ended up going to work with her hair still wet from the shower. She rarely wore makeup, but that was more due to the fact that it took too long to apply it than any protest against major makeup companies. If she skipped makeup, she could spend five or ten more minutes in bed. Getting the extra rest was always preferable to spending time in front of the mirror.

Her bed was decorated with several stuffed animals. She liked aquatic animals and after she'd make her bed, she would carefully place them over the pillows. There was a dolphin, a seal, a whale and a couple of brightly colored fish. I still have them and one of the fish has a note on the tag that says "To: Lynn Love From: Shawn." Shawn would play jokes on Lynn by moving the stuffed aquatic animals around the room when she wasn't looking.

Lynn knew a lot about sharks, dolphins and whales. She'd been on a whale watch about a month before she died and was disappointed to find there were very few whales to watch. Her video collection included *National Geographic* tapes with documentaries on dolphins, killer whales, and great white sharks. She once told me that if you ever get circled by a shark, the best thing to do is lie still because they like to bite things that move around a lot just to see if they can eat them. While it was sound advice, I hope to never test it in the ocean.

While she had a few stuffed animals as decoration, she kept one in particular as a good luck charm. She kept a small purple bull in her car. She called him "Bully" which was something she got from another cartoon show she enjoyed, *Dr. Katz, Professional Therapist.* The main character's son, Ben, kept a small stuffed bull as a security blanket (even though Ben was twenty-four years old). Lynn had her own Bully in her car, as a "safety precaution." I still have Bully at my house but I'm not really sure what to do with him.

Lynn had a good work ethic. She had big plans for her life. She wanted to be the president of a company by the time she was forty. Her plan included not necessarily working for a large company. I am a writer and have written several screenplays. Lynn and I discussed starting a production company and she said I could do whatever I wanted: produce, direct, write, and etc. She insisted that I could do any of those things as long as she was the president of the company.

That was only one part of her entrepreneurial spirit. She also talked about running a company that helped people organize big events. She liked the idea of coordinating a trade show of some sort and it was something she planned to look into later in her life.

She was likable. She took the extra step for people and they all always recognized that. After she was killed, my family received copies of emails Lynn had sent to people who just wanted us to see the kinds of things she had done for them. Some people that worked with her wanted us to know how much they appreciated a simple gesture like opening the door for people. When her office was moved, she ended up near a busy door that was always locked. Many times a day, she got up from her desk to let people in. It may seem small, but several people wanted us to know the extent that they appreciated it, because she could easily have pretended not to hear them knocking.

For a person with serious dreams and serious plans, she joked around quite a bit. She liked to keep a smile on her face and on those around her. Sometimes this could be annoying, because not all of us are in a good mood all day. But you can't get mad at someone for trying to make you smile, can you?

Both Lynn and Shawn liked to travel. Between them, they had traveled all over the world. In the last couple of years of their lives they'd been to England, France, Germany and Australia to name a few places. In the last nine months of their lives, they flew four separate times. Lynn and Shawn went to Palm Beach Garden, Florida in January of 2001. They were in England for Valentine's Day in the February of 2001. They went to Disney World in Florida in the summer of 2001. They lost their lives attempting to go to Hawaii in September of 2001. You can see that they were a couple who didn't just talk about going somewhere and seeing something. They went out and did it.

They swam with the dolphins in Australia. They drank in the pubs in England. They celebrated a wedding in Germany. They had their pictures taken at various tourist attractions in France. Shawn actually lived on three different continents in his short lifetime. There is absolutely no telling what the two of them would have done and what things they might have experienced if the chance hadn't been taken away from them in such a violent way.

Like the rest of us, they weren't perfect. They did the best they could to live happy and productive lives. Sure they had bad days like everyone. They had the ability to get angry at people. We so often hear about people who seem to become overnight saints when they die. So, no, they weren't saints. But I think we'd all do better by trying to live our lives more like they did.

How do you sum up their lives? How can I explain the hole left behind when Lynn was taken from me? You can look at all that has happened since they died and you can see how special they were. There have been many memorials, trees, stones, and even a giant man-made waterfall. A star has been named after Lynn. People in the small town of Belmont, Mississippi erected a flagpole in honor of a girl they never met. We have had dinner dances and raffles in memory of Lynn and Shawn. We've had golf tournaments to raise money for a scholarship fund in her honor. The scholarship fund has thus far helped three students pay for school and raised over one hundred twenty thousand dollars in just a three year period (and we're not done yet). We can rest assured kids will be getting a chance at college for many years to come.

Lynn has inspired as many people since she died as she did when she was alive. No one will ever forget her, I am very sure of that.

Least of all, me.

The church was packed to beyond capacity for her memorial service. Following the service, I had to gather myself together before I could go outside because I knew the cameras were rolling. The press was waiting. Although I still wasn't talking I did take the opportunity to hold an American flag up to the rows of photographers. A friend of mine saw it and said it broke his heart and healed it at the same time. If the image wasn't burned into his memory he only needed to look at the newspaper the next day, because for the second time inside of a week, I made the front page.

I wasn't the only one with an American flag that day. We all had them as we drove through the center of North Attleborough. People lined the sidewalks on both sides of the street to show their support. Main roads were blocked off, giving us the right of way. Police saluted the car as the procession passed by them. Veterans, in full uniform, also saluted us as we drove by. As sad as I was, I couldn't help but feel pride in my country. In the face of tragedy, people pulled together as they almost always do. A small act can go such a long way. People I never met before made us feel a little better about ourselves.

I miss her every day of my life and never a moment goes by when I'm not comparing myself to her memory. Is this or that something she would approve? What can I do to honor her, to preserve her legacy? How can all of us be better people. How can we turn this tragedy into a step towards world peace?

It's easy, really.

Just live more like Lynn and Shawn did.

PICTURES

LEFT: Lynn and her brother at the Tavern From Tower Square in Plainville, MA. This picture was taken when the restaurant re-opened. The function rooms downstairs were dedicated to Lynn and Shawn by the restaurant's owners: Kevin and Eileen Hodgman and David and Eileen Miller.

RIGHT: Lynn and Taylar at a cousin's wedding reception. As children, Lynn and Taylar looked like sisters. In fact, they looked so much alike that when Taylar was walking by the house with her grandfather (when she was two years old) Lynn's mother ran to her crib to be certain it wasn't Lynn out there.

LEFT: Lynn and Taylar at two years old. Taylar is on the left and Lynn is looking at the camera.

ABOVE: This picture was taken September 11, 2002 in New York City at about two-thirty in the morning. From left, Christina Conry, Neil Goodchild and Katie Nicoloro. This is the first time Neil went to Ground Zero. His parents went to see the wreckage in 2001, but he declined the offer. The Twin Towers should be standing directly across from them in this picture.

BELOW: Septemebr 11, 2003. The Goodchild family, Neil, Ellen and Bill are standing in the street in front of their home in Attleboro, MA. The truck behind them is part of the Attleboro Fire Department's fleet. It is painted like an American flag and features a logo honoring the heroes of September 11th which you can see above Bill's head in this picture.